modern
elementary
science

modern elementary science

Abraham S. Fischler
Samuel S. Blanc
Mary Nicholas Farley
Lawrence F. Lowery
Vincent E. Smith

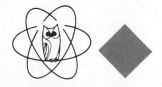

HOLT, RINEHART AND WINSTON, INC.
New York   Toronto   London   Sydney

Authors

Dr. Abraham S. Fischler is James Donn Professor of Education, Dean of Graduate Studies and Director of the Social and Behavioral Sciences Center at Nova University in Fort Lauderdale, Florida. Dr. Fischler has co-authored numerous elementary and Junior High School science textbooks and has also written extensively in a great many science journals and bulletins over the past fifteen years.

Dr. Sam Blanc is Associate Professor of Education at the San Diego State College and was a classroom teacher for nineteen years. He was the science Coordinator of Junior High Schools for eight years in the Denver School System and Director of Science and Math at Cajon Valley School District in California. Dr. Blanc has written numerous books and articles in science education.

Mary Nicholas Farley is the Dean of Women and Lecturer in Education and Physics at Georgian Court College in Lakewood, New Jersey. Sister Mary Nicholas has taught elementary school science and was then Elementary School Principal for twelve years. She has also written a number of elementary school science programs and has been a consultant in education in a wide variety of innovative educational programs.

Dr. Lawrence F. Lowery is the Testing Teacher and Evaluator for Elementary School Science Projects at the University of California. He has authored numerous elementary school science books for children and has written a great many science articles for elementary school teachers. Dr. Lowery was formerly a Teacher—Principal in the Oakland Unified School District in Oakland, California.

Dr. Vincent Edward Smith is teaching full time at Sarah Lawrence College, preparing a book-length manuscript on the history of the laws of nature and is an Associate at Columbia University. Dr. Smith has co-authored an entire elementary school science series and has authored numerous publications and articles in journals and encyclopedias.

Consultants

Dr. Lyman C. Hunt, Jr. is Professor of Education and Director of the Reading Center at the University of Vermont. Dr. Hunt has taught elementary school and has published several journal articles on reading. He has addressed numerous educational organizations and interested civic groups across the nation on the subject of reading.

Dr. John N. Shive is Manager of Science Lectures and Demonstrations of Bell Telephone Laboratories, Inc. Dr. Shive is the author of three textbooks in Physics, specializing in wave behavior and electronics. He has written high school science articles, and has given lectures for various educational and civic groups.

Mr. Leonard Simon is the Acting Assistant Director of the Bureau of Curriculum Development in New York City. He has taught mathematics on both the Junior High and Senior High School level. Mr. Simon has instructed at such schools as New York University, Bronx Community College, and City College of New York. Mr. Simon has also written a number of elementary mathematics books for young children and is the co-author of a highly successful elementary school mathematics program.

Dr. Walter Steidle is the Chief of the Program Development Section for elementary and secondary education, for the United States Office of Education. He was the State Supervisor for the State of Delaware and became top specialist of Science for the United States Office of Education. Dr. Steidle has written numerous magazine articles on elementary school science, and was given the honor of being awarded the title of Congressional Fellow from 1968-69.

Dr. Joel Warren is Professor of Life Sciences at Nova University in Fort Lauderdale, Florida. He has occupied various University teaching positions over the past thirty years. Professor Warren has written numerous articles in the general fields of microbiology and infectious diseases.

Illustrated by

Tim and Greg Hildebrandt
Dave Hodges
Richard Loehle
Raul Mina Mora

Contents

vi

unit one
Animals, Plants,
and Places

You are familiar with plants and animals. But have you ever noticed the place in which they live? Have you ever thought that there might be a link between living things and their surroundings? Let's look at a certain place and a particular animal, the peppered moth, living in it.

The peppered moth lives near the industrial city of Manchester, England. Before 1845, the moth was light colored with some dark spots. Birds, the moth's enemy, had difficulty seeing it as the moth rested on light tree bark. The color of the moth helped it blend in with its surroundings. In 1845, however, a black peppered moth was captured. It was a new variety. Could the black moth live in light-colored surroundings?

Manchester was rapidly becoming an industrial center, and factory chimney soot had darkened the grey tree bark. Black moths resting on this bark were hard to find, and birds found the light moths were easier to see and eat. Within fifty years almost all kinds of peppered moths in the area of Manchester were of the black variety.

Animals and plants are suited to the places in which they live. These places are called habitats (HAB-i-tats). Many animals and plants must live in special places where they can obtain food and water, where they can protect themselves, and where they can reproduce.

Some animals are more at home in forests, while others are most at home in open fields. Think of some plants and animals you find on a desert. Can you name some plants and animals that live only in water? Would a cow eat the same food as a tiger? Why can some animals live in cold places while others cannot?

You will be studying animals and plants in their surroundings. There are many ways that animals and plants are suited to live in fields or in woods, on mountains, or on deserts, and in fresh water. Each plant or animal lives in the habitat that is best for it.

WHAT ARE SOME HABITATS OF LIVING THINGS?

Some of your observations of plants and animals can be done at home or in the classroom. Dogs and cats are common pets. You probably would not bring a pet to school, but you can study it at home. What other animals besides dogs and cats do people keep as pets?

What differences do you notice between cats and dogs? Are all dogs alike? How do they differ? Are all cats alike? How are they different? Find out what cats eat. Find out what dogs eat.

4

1/Observe

Make a list in your notebook of different kinds of pets as shown in the following table.

Kind of Pet	Body Covering	Kind of Food
1. Dog	Fur	Meat
2. Cat	Fur	Meat, Fish
3.		
4.		
5.		

Do plants also differ in how they look? Do they all need the same care? Do most plants you know grow better in bright sun? Do some plants grow better in shade?

2/Compare

Collect some leaves from different plants. Draw their outlines. Observe how they differ in size and shape. Are there any similarities? ■

Observing plants and animals can be an exciting experience in your classroom. Let us make a typical plant and animal habitat in the following activity.

3/Investigate

A field terrarium in your classroom is a good place for observing the habits of some small animals. An empty fish tank will make a good container. First, put a layer of small pebbles about an inch deep in the bottom. Now place a half-inch layer of sand over the pebbles. Finish with an inch of garden-rich soil.

Collect your plants from a wooded area. You can get low-growing plants like ferns, mosses, and other small plants. Leave some of the soil around the roots when you dig up ferns or mosses. Keep the soil moist around the plant roots until you have planted them in the terrarium.

Water your terrarium well. The water should be about halfway up the layer of pebbles. Keep your terrarium almost completely covered with a glass plate. This covering will help to conserve the moisture needed by the plants, and they will not have to be watered as often.

Now your terrarium is ready for some animals. A toad, if you can get one, is an interesting animal to observe. You can feed it earthworms. How does the toad eat? A toad's tongue is sticky. Watch the action of the tongue as you feed an earthworm to the toad. You may want to get other animals for your terrarium. A frog, small garter snake, salamander, or a turtle also makes a good terrarium pet. Find out what kind of food your terrarium animal will need. Why should you not put too many animals in your terrarium? ■

In order to keep plants and animals alive in your classroom, you must try to provide the things they would have in their natural habitat. A frog in your terrarium would need a small pan of water so that it could keep its skin moist. If you were growing plants that should have a lot of sun, you would place them on a window sill instead of in a shady place. Since cactus plants grow naturally in the desert, would they need much water? In each case you try to make the new habitat as much like the natural one as possible.

TESTING YOUR IDEAS

A cactus was planted in rich, brown soil, shaded from the sun, and watered twice a day. The cactus died. Which of the following reasons best explains why the plant died?

A cactus may die of a disease.
A cactus usually has a short life.
A cactus never survives outside of a desert.
A cactus usually can only live and grow in a habitat which meets its needs.

WHAT IS THE KIND OF HABITAT IN WHICH YOU LIVE?

You can continue your study of living things and their surroundings near your home or school. If there are fields or open lots nearby, you might find some wild flowers and grasses. Do you know what we usually call these wild flowers and grasses? If you say they are weeds, you are correct! Since weeds are growing in their natural habitat, they grow very fast. If you have a garden, you pull out the weeds to protect the plants you are trying to grow. Name some other places where you have observed weeds growing.

Walking through a field, you may see a rabbit hop quickly through the grass and then stop to eat. What does a rabbit eat? There will be food and shelter for each kind of animal you find in the field.

Under an upturned stone you may see fat, white worms, called grubs. These are young beetles. In a moist area, you might find salamanders or earthworms. Take a look under a large rock. You can study the plants and animals living in your schoolyard, an empty lot, in a park, or small open area. Let us see how many plants and animals we find in one area.

4/Observe

Before you go out into the area, you should be organized into teams. Decide what each team will look for. Several animals can be assigned to each team. There may be insects, spiders, sparrows, toads, squirrels, cats, chipmunks, rabbits, and many other animals in the open area you select for study. Other teams will look for plants such as trees, shrubs, grasses, ferns and mosses. The captain of each team will record the name and number of the animals and plants that his team finds. ■

Looking for plants and animals needs careful observation. When first going out to look, you may think there is little to find. Upturned rocks might reveal tiny insects. Ant hills may be found when you brush aside grass. Careful looking is the key to a successful hunt.

On your next field trip you could select one animal for study. The squirrel is one of the most common animals around many homes or in parks in certain parts of the United States. So many of these furry animals live in city parks that many of them are almost as tame as dogs or cats. Even if these park squirrels were not fed peanuts and popcorn, they would not grow hungry. They are well suited for finding the food they need. Look at the picture of the squirrel. What do you think it can eat? Note the shape of its teeth.

When you spot a squirrel, watch to see what food it is collecting or eating. Notice how it climbs a tree. Could you climb a tree that fast? How do its sharp claws help the squirrel? What use to the squirrel is its bushy tail as it jumps from one branch to another?

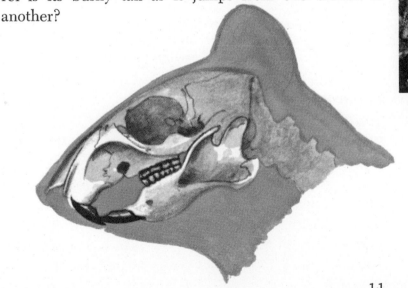

5/Observe

You may want to observe a bird, a kitten or some other familiar animal. Write down the observations you make of the animal you select for study. Describe the size, shape and color of the animal. How many legs does it have? Do any animals use their legs for something besides moving? Notice the food an animal eats. Find out where the animal spends most of its time. ■

TESTING YOUR IDEAS

Which of the following statements are true about the area in which you live?

The area in which you live is a particular habitat.

Your area has special habitats in it, such as an empty lot, a woods; a park, pond or garden; an apartment house, a home; a flower pot, fish tank, or bird cage.

Your area is part of a larger habitat.

The weather in your area is practically the same all year round.

There are many kinds of animals and plants in the area in which you live.

The kinds of animals in your area are the same whatever the time of year.

WHAT LIVES IN THE HABITAT
OF A POND?

You will be able to observe and study hundreds of living things if you live near a freshwater pond, a small stream, or near a park which has a body of water where living things might grow. Ask an adult to go with you. Each time you go exploring you will discover something interesting and new. Pond exploring can be an adventure. The kinds of plants and animals you discover will depend on the size of the pond, its location, how deep it is, and many other conditions. The plants and animals you find may be different from those your classmates find in other ponds.

An ordinary pond is a small body of water fed by a small stream or spring. Its edges are overgrown by plants whose roots grow in the moist soil or mud. Most ponds are not very deep. Some plants grow in the water at the pond's edge. Still other plants are able to grow on and beneath the surface of the pond.

Since pond life is always changing with the seasons, the time of year you decide to visit a pond is important. What is a good time to explore a pond in the region where you live? What is the poorest time of the year? In many parts of our country, the first sign of spring is the appearance of skunk cabbage

along the banks of ponds and streams. Cattails and other plants rise out of the shallow water where their roots are anchored in the muddy bottom. Farther out from the shore, duckweed and pond lillies float on the surface of the water.

There are many places for animals to hide and many sources of food in ponds. Can you think where tadpoles, salamanders and insects searching for food might be hiding? In trying to obtain food, many animals are in danger of being eaten themselves. All these pond dwellers are carrying on a battle to stay alive.

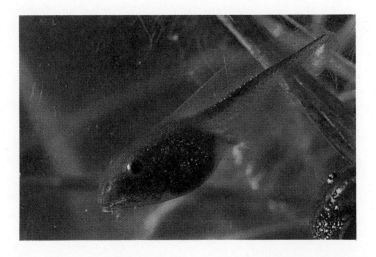

Think of some ways in which changes of season might cause pond life to become different.

Cold, rain, periods of dry weather, chemicals in the water, and changes of season can affect pond life.

Why do some scientists study plants and animals in their natural habitats? Why is it sometimes necessary to collect samples of plants and animals for further study indoors? You may want to study some pond animals in your classroom by doing the next activity.

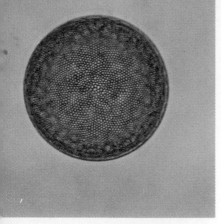

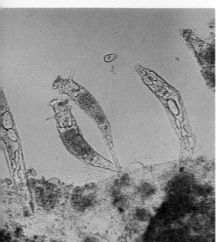

6/Investigate

Walk along the edge of a pond or any other shallow body of fresh water. Look for some duckweed, as is shown in the picture, or a small, flowering plant. They are usually found in quiet, sheltered, shoreline areas. Collect some of the plant and some of the water below it. Use a jar which you can cover with a lid. With your teacher's help, examine the water with a microscope or microprojector. Do you find any tiny animals among the plant? Do you see any of them clinging to the roots? How does the plant help these animals breathe? When you collected the plant, did you see any animals that might eat the creatures that you found? Why is the plant a good habitat for these living things? ■

The variety of animals found in a pond may be great. It may range from those that can be seen only with a magnifier to those as large as fish. Your collection will be just a small sampling of pond animals.

Walking along the shore of most ponds in spring or summer, you can hear and see frogs splashing in the water. Some pond frogs have bright green heads and darker green backs. Their bellies are white, and the throats of the male frogs are often bright yellow. Can you explain why the coloring of a frog helps it hide from its enemies?

Frogs play an important part in pond life. Like many other pond animals, frogs go through many body changes during their lives. Frogs start as tiny eggs covered with a jelly-like covering. These eggs can be

found among the water plants of the pond in the spring
or early summer. The dark spots in the jelly mass are
frog eggs from which tadpoles will grow.

Tadpoles live like fish during their early lives. They
have gills and can get oxygen they need from the pond
water. In the next few weeks the tadpoles will grow
legs, develop lungs, and gradually lose their tails. They
develop from the tadpole stage into frogs.

Tadpoles feed on small plants in water. They can
be called vegetarians (veh-juh-TAIR-ee-unz) because
they eat only plants. If you can catch some tadpoles
and observe them in your classroom, you can see what
they eat. Put some water plants into your aquarium.
Tadpoles will also eat small pieces of lettuce.

Put some of your tadpoles in the aquarium with
bigger fish. What do you think will happen to some of
the tadpoles? The diet of tadpoles changes as they

grow larger. When they change into frogs, they eat earthworms, caterpillars, and insects.

Is the animal and plant life in streams like that in ponds? It may change more in streams since pond water moves less. There are many kinds of freshwater fish found in streams. Trout fishing in a stream is a great sport for fishermen. Sometimes streams are blocked by beavers building dams. How do you think such dams might affect plant and animal life in streams? Would the seasons change life in streams? How does plant and animal life differ as the temperature of their habitat becomes higher or lower?

TESTING YOUR IDEAS

Which of the following statements best explains why a pond is a special habitat?

A pond is a place where animals and plants live and grow.
Animal life in a pond battles to stay alive.
In a pond, there are many different kinds of plants.
Some animals and plants are not likely to be found anywhere else except in a pond or pond-like habitat.

WHAT ANIMALS AND PLANTS
LIVE IN THE SEA?

Salt water is the home of many animals that could not live in a freshwater pond habitat. There are shellfish that are interesting to study along the ocean shoreline. These are animals with soft bodies that are protected by hard coverings or shells. Such animals make their shells as they grow.

Have you ever eaten oysters or clams? Do you know what a living oyster or clam looks like? If you live near a seashore, finding shellfish on the beach is an interesting experience. Be sure to visit the seashore when the tide is low and the plants and animals living in that kind of habitat are not covered with water. Check in the rocky or muddy areas.

7/Describe

Oysters and clams remain in one spot instead of moving around. The shells of oysters are rough and bumpy. Do these shells look like anything you have ever seen before? How do you think an oyster or clam gets its food since it doesn't move from place to place?

Try to open a clam or oyster. Why are the shells so difficult to open? When you eat scallops, clams, or oysters, you are eating some of the strong muscles that hold together the two halves of the animal's shells. How do such muscles protect these shellfish? ■

The soft-bodied hermit crab may also be found near the seashore. It doesn't make its own shell. The crab finds an empty snail shell and crawls into it. If

21

you know what a hermit is, decide whether these crabs are well named. Starfish and brightly colored sea urchins covered with prickly spines are seashore dwellers. Of what use are its spines to the sea urchin?

Sea animals are well adapted to their natural habitat. Often their structure is such that enemies are discouraged from eating or attacking them. How would a starfish repel its enemies?

The plants that are most common in the ocean are so small that they can be seen only with a microscope. These tiny plants are algae (AL-jee). Free-floating algae and microscopic animals form plankton (PLANK-tun). Which animals do you think live on plankton? Would you believe that a whale uses plankton as food?

Some algae are anchored to rocks and sand. They grow into large plants, called kelps (KELPS). The kelps have stems as long as 100 feet. Air bladders on the stalks of these plants keep the kelps afloat in the water. Most algae plants are green, but some varieties of kelps are red or brown.

23

The turtle in the photograph lives in the sea. A sea turtle has legs that are flattened like paddles. What is the difference between the sea turtle and the land turtle? When sea turtles are ready to lay eggs they come out of the water and onto the land. Then they return to the sea. Later on, the newly hatched turtles find their way to the ocean.

On the ocean floor are flat fish that are very specially suited to living in this habitat. The flounder in the picture is such a flat fish. The upper side of its body is dark like the floor of the ocean. How is this coloring helpful to the flounder? Do you know where the eyes are in a flounder? If you say on both sides of the head, you are wrong! Both eyes are on one side, the upper side of the fish. The flounder swims in a strange way with its body tilted to one side. How do you think this way of swimming is helpful to the flounder?

When the young flounder is hatched from the egg, it swims like any normal young fish. Its eyes are

24

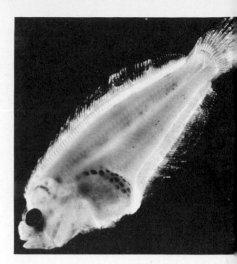

on opposite sides of its head. When the young fish is about one inch long, one of its eyes begins to change its position. For example, the eye on the right side of the fish's head will move across to the left side, until both eyes are on the same side. This strange movement takes only about three or four days.

How many other plants and animals do you know that are especially fitted for life in the ocean?

TESTING YOUR IDEAS

With which of the following statements do you agree?

The sea is a good home for any kind of water animal or plant.

The sea turtle, kelp, and flounder are all entirely different living things and have nothing in common at all.

The sea is like a pond, because both are particular habitats.

The sea is like the area in which you live, because both have special habitats within them.

Some seas are warmer than others. But the animals and plants in these different seas are the same in kind.

WHAT PLANTS AND ANIMALS LIVE ON MOUNTAINS?

Have you ever climbed or driven up a high mountain? It might have been one of the great mountains in the western part of the United States. Did you feel any change in the temperature as you traveled higher? Did you see regions in which the plants were different colors along the way up?

When you stand at the foot of a high mountain and look up, you will see regions of different colors. There may be several shades of green, brown, and gray.

Some of the highest mountains in North America are white on the top because they are capped with snow. This snow does not melt even in the summertime. When traveling up such a mountain, you can see that the changing colors mark off different parts of the mountain, which we call life zones. How do you think the different climates might affect the plants and animals living on the mountain?

At the foot of the mountain there may be fields with much green grass. Forests of oak, pine, and evergreen surround these fields. Animals, such as chipmunks and rabbits, may be running about looking for food. Different kinds of birds can also be seen.

Higher up on the mountain, the deeper green color that you noticed from the bottom of the mountain is made by forests of tall evergreen trees. Large pine cones may be scattered over the ground. Gophers run out of their burrows. Fish may be found in a pool of water fed by a mountain stream. The black and brown bears on this part of the mountain may catch fish for their next meal, or they may look for berries and nuts.

27

Farther up, there are rugged cliffs. Small plants, with long, thin roots can grow in the cracks of these rocks. Mountain goats live on this rocky land. How do their small feet help them? Would the trees on this part of the mountain be tall or short? Why?

No trees will grow above a certain height on a mountain. There is a definite line where the trees end. This height is called the timberline. From the timberline to the top of the mountain, the rocky slopes are often covered with snow much of the year. Even so, there are animals that live on this part of the mountain. Small birds called finches eat insects and seeds that the wind blows onto the snow. Other birds, such as the mountain chickadee and the junco in the Rockies, nest at the top of the mountains. They move down in the wintertime to the foothills.

Gather pictures of the animals and plants you might see if you traveled up a peak of a high mountain. Make a notebook of them and divide them into those you would expect to see at the various life zones on the mountain. Describe some of the animals and plants. Which are the different animals and plants found at different levels?

What do you think determines where particular plants and animals live? The living things found at various mountain levels must be able to survive the conditions present at the level at which they live.

Why is the climate at the top of a very high mountain like that at the North Polar region? Can you name animals at this polar region that you would not find on a mountain?

TESTING YOUR IDEAS

With which of the following statements do you agree?

A mountain is one kind of habitat with only one kind of climate.

Animals and plants which live near or on a mountain usually can live on any part of it.

A mountain is a good habitat for any kind of animal or plant.

Since a mountain is a habitat, it is like the area in which you live, or a pond, or the sea.

HOW DO ANIMALS AND PLANTS LIVE IN OTHER REGIONS?

Polar bears are the largest land animals of the North Polar region. They live in icy regions the year round, but they are well suited for living in such cold lands. These animals have very thick coats of fur. Polar bears have a layer of fat under their skin which also helps to keep in the heat of their bodies. These bears are good swimmers and can swim in the cold arctic waters. They can withstand the freezing temperatures because of their heavy coat of oily fur and the fat layer underneath. The polar bear has heavy pads of fur on the soles of its feet. How would this fur help the polar bear walk over ice without slipping? Would you like to see what a polar habitat looks like? Let's do the next activity to find out.

8/Compare

Bring in a cardboard box. Paint the inside of the box white, the color of a polar habitat. Now cut out paper animals living in this habitat. Color them so they will blend in with the background. How does the color of an animal help it in its natural habitat? ■

If it were not for the blending in of many animals with the colors of their habitat, they would have a very difficult time escaping enemies or approaching their prey. Animals which have colors adapted to their habitat have been able to survive better than those that did not. Do you now understand why most polar bears have white fur? How does this color help the polar bear? This animal lives mostly on seals and fish, but polar bears also eat birds and foxes. Some of these animals are as white as the polar bear. Arctic foxes are white. An arctic bird, called the ptarmigan (TAR-mi-gan), has white feathers in the winter but gets brown feathers in the spring. Do you think food is hard to find in winter at the polar regions? Why must meat-eating polar animals be skillful hunters?

Although there are no trees at the North Pole, there are some familiar plants growing there. Mosses and other small plants are able to grow in these cold arctic regions.

Why do you think animals and plants living in very dry land areas are usually very different from those that live on mountains, at the North Pole, or in fields? To survive all living things must have water. Since deserts have very little rainfall, do you think that desert animals and plants must have special ways of finding and saving water?

Camels can live without water for several days and sometimes as long as a month. They are well adapted to life in the desert. A thirsty camel may drink 20 gallons of water at one time. The camel can store this water in its muscles. Do you think the camel stores water in its hump? This thought is a common error. The hump on a camel's back is fat which is used as stored food.

Camels sometimes get water, as well as food, from plants such as cactus, which grow well in a desert habitat. What type of roots would these plants have? Why are the stems of the cactus so large?

A camel can walk over the soft hills of sand easily with its large, spongy and flat feet. This animal has long, thick eyelashes, and slit-shaped nostrils that can be closed tightly. How would these be useful to a camel in a sandstorm? A camel is able to get along in its desert habitat because its body is adapted to desert conditions.

One of the best known North American plains animals is the coyote (KY-oht). The coyote is a member of the wolf family. It is a good hunter and will eat rabbits, mice, ground squirrels, lizards, snakes, birds, and insects. It may also live on cactus and the beans of the mesquite (mes-KEET) plant when other food is scarce.

The mesquite, like the cactus, is specially suited to desert life. In Death Valley, California, mesquite plants have roots 30 to 100 feet long. Why are such long roots needed? How do the long roots of some desert plants help desert animals?

9/Describe

Use pictures to make a notebook of animals that live on the deserts of North America. What plants live there? How is each plant and animal fitted to live in this dry climate? ■

The important adaptations that desert plants and animals have enable them to make use of the little water present. Each variety of desert life has its special structure to make this water adaptation. You can see such structures in the animals and plants if you make a desert terrarium.

10/Observe

First, get a few small cactus plants, some sand, and a large fishbowl. Put a layer of garden soil into the fishbowl before adding the sand. Add a sand layer of about two inches and place your cactus plants in it. A horned toad or salamander will be a suitable animal for your terrarium. The cactus will not need to be watered more than once a week. Provide a small pan of water and some live ants or other small insects to take care of the food needs of your terrarium animal. ◼

Your terrarium is intended to provide desert conditions for the plants and animals within it. Therefore, you should provide the animals with live food such as flies. Toads and snakes prefer such food. If you cannot find live food for the toad, use small bits of meat. Man-made habitats should follow closely the ones nature provides.

Some animals live in underground burrows and dens. Foxes, wolves, skunks, coyotes, and prairie dogs are among such animals. Even an owl might nest in the empty burrow of a skunk or fox. Burrowing animals in the desert may live underground during the hot day and come out to hunt for food at night. What might be some other reasons why animals build underground homes?

Fox dens may be as deep as 10 feet underground. The cubs are born there. The den has a storage room and a lookout place. Why must the fox be on the lookout for other animals?

Ants have more unusual underground nests than most animals. There are so many skilled workers among ants that they can have nests with many rooms that are connected by tunnels. Some ants build roads and tunnels. Other ants are like woodworkers and carve passages through pieces of wood.

Other ants may be like farmers. Some of them grow plants to feed the colony. One kind of ant milks plant sap from insects called aphids (AY-fids). Aphids suck the sap from plants. When stroked by an ant, the aphid gives a drop of plant sap in a form called honeydew.

11/Observe

You can watch ants in a colony. Get a shovel and a gallon jar and begin to dig around an ant hill. Fill half the jar with loose soil. Dig at least a foot deep

into the side of the ant hill. Scoop up the dirt and pick out the ants and their eggs. If you see a very large ant, be sure to capture it for your colony. This is the queen ant. Put the ants and the eggs into the jar. Cover the jar with a cloth held by a rubber band. Why would it be wrong to cap the jar with a metal lid?

Wrap heavy black cloth or paper around the bottom half of the jar to keep out sunlight. The ants will then build their tunnels against the side of the jar. Unwrap the jar each day and observe the ants.

Food crumbs and a few drops of water should be added every few days. Put a small piece of candy in the jar. Note how long it is before the first ant finds the candy. How much time did it take for the second ant to find it? Do you think ants let each other know about food in the jar? ■

Ants work so closely together that we call them social animals. They divide the colony into kinds of ants who have specific jobs. For such simple animals they build very fine colonies. Ants are strong and can move objects many times their weight.

TESTING YOUR IDEAS

Which of the following statements is true?

Forests, ponds, seas, mountains, the polar regions, deserts, and plains are all the habitats there are.

There are as many habitats as there are places where living things may live and grow.

HOW DO SOME ANIMALS SURVIVE SEASONAL CHANGE?

Nature comes back to life in the springtime in most areas. There is a great change in the appearance of things after the cold winter is over. What are some of the changes you can see in trees and bushes from day to day as the weather gets warmer? You could make a bulletin board display of some of the signs of spring. What is happening as these changes are taking place?

During the spring season dogs and cats gradually lose their thick winter coats of fur. In the far north ptarmigans and snowshoe rabbits change their white winter coats to brown spring ones. Birds leave their winter homes and fly north. Some song birds also change their colors. Male birds usually grow brighter-colored feathers. What do you think may be the reason for this color change? After the male bird finds a mate, he often helps the female build a nest and care for the young birds.

Frogs and fish become more active in the spring. Turtles and snakes begin looking for good places to lay their eggs. Why do they lay their eggs at this time of the year?

Moths, butterflies, and other insects appear again in the spring. How many different kinds of insects can you find? What appears to be the most important factor in bringing about the changes of spring? Explain how warm weather affects you. Did you know that crickets are fairly good thermometers? They chirp more rapidly as the weather gets warmer. When the weather gets very hot or fairly cold, they do not chirp at all. You can observe crickets in the next activity.

12/Compare

Get a large fishbowl or other container. Put about two inches of loose dirt in the bottom of the bowl. Put 10 or 15 adult crickets in the bowl. If you cannot find crickets, you can buy them at a store that sells fishing bait.

Put some water in the lid of a small jar for the crickets. Place a piece of sponge in the lid so they

will not drown in the water. Put pieces of apple and lettuce in the bowl for the crickets to eat. Cover the top of the bowl with a cloth. Tie a string around the mouth of the bowl to keep the cloth in place. Now place your cricket bowl in a pan of ice cubes. Wait several minutes until the cricket bowl cools. What do you notice happening as the bowl gets colder and colder?

Put the bowl near a radiator or heater. Do the crickets chirp when they get very warm? Get a thermometer and measure the temperature at which the crickets stop chirping. Cover the cricket bowl with a dark cloth. Do the crickets chirp in the dark? ■

It was once thought that the chirping of crickets was due to their rubbing their legs together. After careful observation it was found that the chirping was due to the rapid beating of their wings. They do rub their legs together, but this rubbing does not cause the chirping.

Cold weather causes some animals to become inactive. Others are affected by the hot weather. The ground hog and the woodchuck are among the animals that sleep through the long, cold winter. This resting in winter is called hibernation (hy-ber-NAY-shun).

A hibernating animal is like an animal in deep sleep. But there are some differences. Its heart beats very slowly. Its body temperature is lowered and it breathes very little. Many frogs, too, sleep through the cold winter. If you can get a frog, you can cause it to become sluggish by lowering its body temperature. To see what happens, let's do the next activity.

Put a frog in a jar. Punch air holes in the lid. Add a small amount of water to the jar to keep the frog's skin moist. Place the jar in the refrigerator over night, but not in the freezer. Notice the frog's movements when you remove the jar from the refrigerator. How long is it before the frog begins to move at all? Put the frog on its back and touch it gently. Is the frog able to get up? Record how long it takes the frog to become active. ■

Doctors have been able to perform some new operations on human beings because they can lower the temperature of the body. The lowered body temperature helps the doctors perform delicate operations they could not otherwise do. The lowered temperature causes the body functions to slow down much the same way as the frog's.

The winter sleep of a bear is somewhat different from hibernation. The bear's breathing and heartbeat slow down, but its body temperature remains high. If the weather is mild, the bear may wake up in mid-winter and then go back to sleep until spring.

Man, too, must sleep. He usually sleeps part of every day. Is his sleep like that of the bear? Do you think man's temperature drops when he sleeps? Do you think his heartbeat slows down? Would man's digestion almost stop, the way a bear's does?

Man does not hibernate, but scientists are hoping that he may in the future. Doctors, as we mentioned before, can slow down a man's heartbeat and his breathing by cooling his body. This slowing down is done in order to make brain and heart operations less dangerous to the patient. Perhaps, if man can be made to

43

hibernate, he could travel into outer space with less food, water, and air than he would need if he were awake and moving around. It will take many years of traveling for man to reach some of the other planets. It would not be such a tiring journey if he could hibernate along the way.

Some animals will pass the summer in a sleepy state. This resting in summer is called estivation (ess-tuh-VAY-shun). Snails and frogs may become inactive or estivate when the weather is very hot.

Some reptiles also may behave in the same way. The ground squirrel of Southern California both estivates and hibernates. This little animal may begin resting in July and sometimes remains this way until the following spring. How might this long rest help the squirrel?

Plants, too, go through periods of inactivity. Some appear to be dead during the winter. We call the plant's seasonal inactivity dormancy (DAWR-mun-see).

Many plants shoot up in the springtime. Where are they during the winter? Do all of them come from seeds? What parts of the plant remain in the soil during the winter months? You will find out about plant dormancy in the following activity.

14/Compare

You can show that there are seeds, roots, and stems in the soil ready to come to life when the weather gets warmer and the soil gets enough moisture. Dig up some rich soil from under dead leaves and put it in a flowerpot. Take out any green plants that are already growing in the soil. Water the dirt in the flowerpot. After about a week look to see if there are any plants growing in the container. Where did they come from?

44

Cut a twig from a flowering tree or bush which hasn't yet bloomed. Keep it in water. What happens? Would the same twig have bloomed if it had been cut last fall and put in water? ■

Taking twigs from flowering shrubs and putting them in water is called forcing. This can be done with plants such as forsythia (for-SITH-ee-uh) and most of the flowering fruit trees. It must be done in spring-time and may take a few weeks for the blossoms to come out.

TESTING YOUR IDEAS

Do you agree with the following statement?

Since a habitat changes with season, and animals and plants change too, animals and plants have adapted to change.

HOW DO OTHER ANIMALS SURVIVE
SEASONAL CHANGE?

Many birds move from one part of the country to another and even from one country to another in the fall and spring. Name the birds that you see around your home all winter. These are called winter residents. What birds return for the spring and summer? These are called summer residents.

Redstarts, cliff swallows, and grosbeaks fly north from Mexico and Central and South America to nest in Canada and the United States. The ruby-throated hummingbird flies across the Gulf of Mexico from Central America back to the eastern part of the United States to nest. Whippoorwills that spend their winter in the southern tip of Florida return to raise their young in New England. Can you figure out how many miles some of these birds fly? Would you like to take such a long trip each year?

Why do you think some people spend their winters in Florida? What makes birds take such long trips? Animals are said to migrate (MY-grayt) when they move in large numbers from one place to a distant place.

Man does not fully understand the reason why birds leave their summer homes and fly hundreds of thousands of miles to another place. When the birds leave the North, there is still plenty of food for them, and the weather has not yet turned cold. We say the birds migrate at a certain time because of an inner urge called instinct (IN-stingkt).

To find out about their patterns of migration scientists trap birds and put bands on their legs. Each band has a number to identify the bird. There are instructions on this band for anyone who captures the bird or finds it dead. If you find such a bird, you are asked to write the Bureau of Biological Survey, U.S. Dept. of Agriculture, telling where you found the bird and the number on its band. By such methods, scientists have found out much information about the migration routes of birds. Can you recognize some of the birds presently in your area?

15/Record

Make a list of birds in your area that are winter residents and a list of those that are summer residents. Do you think that insect-eating birds will be around during the winter? Why not? What do the birds eat during the winter? Why are the birds in your yard different from those in a wooded area? If you wish to observe birds at short range, use the method of "squeaking." To squeak, loudly kiss the back of your hand. Try to remain still. On occasion and particularly during the breeding season, you may find a dozen or more birds will come to inspect the noise you are making. Draw pictures of the birds around your home. Use these for a bulletin board display. To identify birds you cannot easily name, you may with the help of your teacher find them in a book about birds.

You will have to notice the different markings of these birds and their colors to help identify them. Usually the male bird has the brighter colors. Think of why the female would not have brightly-colored feathers. ■

We cannot fully explain migration. One theory says that birds know it is time to migrate when the days begin to shorten in the northern regions. But birds are not the only animals which migrate. It is even harder to explain the migration of some fish, such as the salmon.

Salmon spend years feeding and growing in the ocean. When fully grown, they return to the fresh water where they were hatched. Large numbers of salmon swim up rivers against rapid currents at certain seasons of the year. In their upstream journey they may leap up waterfalls as high as 12 feet. Did you know fish could jump? Measure 12 feet. Can you jump as high as a salmon?

If the salmon successfully make this dangerous trip, the female lays eggs and the male covers them with a whitish fluid from his body called milt (MILT). This act of covering the eggs is called spawning. If we can find out why it is better for salmon eggs to be laid in fresh water, we may discover the reason why these fish make such a difficult journey.

TESTING YOUR IDEAS

Animals migrate from one place to another because a) some animals are travelers b) migration is a means of adapting to surroundings c) all animals at one time or another migrate.

HOW DO OTHER LIVING THINGS CHANGE HABITAT?

Before November 1963, off the southwestern islands of Iceland, there was nothing but the seas of the North Atlantic. But on November 14, 1963, the waters boiled with smoky activity. For almost a year and a half, a fiery birth pushed land above the ocean's surface. An island had risen from the sea about half the size of Central Park in New York City. The island was named Surtsey (SURT-see).

Surtsey had no plant or animal life. Some birds and seals came to use it as a resting place. During the early days of June, however, a scientist found a wonderful thing in the moist soil near the edge of the island's lagoon. A small, green coastal plant called a sea rocket had taken root. Its picture appears on this page. Surtsey was nourishing a living thing, but from where had the sea rocket come? How did it get to the island? An activity will begin to help you answer these questions.

16/Observe

Put some garden soil in a pan. Heat the pan in an oven for one hour at 400°F to kill any plant or animal life present. Then, place the pan outdoors. Continually moisten the soil. Do any insects or animals find their way to the soil? Do you find after several weeks plants growing in the soil? How did the plants get there? Were the plant's seeds carried to the soil by the wind? ■

Some seeds can be carried by wind. The milk-weed seed has little silky hairs growing out of its covering. These tiny hairs are like parachutes that help the seed travel. Cattails, which grow along ponds and streams, also have "flyaway" seeds.

The seed of the sea rocket has no parachute, however. The sea rocket grows along Icelandic shores and can also be found on North American coasts. But its seeds cannot be carried by wind. To reach the shores of Surtsey, the seed had to be carried by water. Accidentally, a seed from a sea rocket, possibly from a nearby island, drifted to Surtsey and took root.

Your activity showed you that wind can carry seeds. The example of Surtsey showed you that water can carry seeds. Animals can carry seeds, too. A bird will pick up a cherry, carry it for some distance, eat the soft part, and then drop the seed. Sometimes animals may migrate from one country to another on ships or airplanes. All of these kinds of migration we call dispersal (dis-PER-sal).

In time, Surtsey will be covered with green plants. Seals, insects, and other animals will come there, too. By dispersal, living things will have changed their old habitat for a new one.

TESTING YOUR IDEAS

Plants change their habitat by means of wind or by being carried by animals. Some animals change their habitat by being carried by ship or airplane. Such a change occurs a) by instinct b) by chance.

HOW ARE LIVING THINGS PROTECTED FROM THEIR ENEMIES?

So far you have studied animals and plants in their physical surroundings. Their physical surroundings also include other living things. Animals and plants must be protected from other living things.

The best means of protection for many animals is their ability to run, fly, or swim quickly. Most birds have no other way to defend themselves. The cottontail rabbit in the eastern part of the United States and the jack rabbit of the western prairies hop so fast that they often get away from dogs or foxes. Swimming is the means used by some animals to escape their enemies. What happens when you try to catch a frog on the side of a pond? How do fish escape dangerous enemies?

Think how horses, tigers, and clams protect themselves. How does a swordfish use its "sword"?

Many animals have their outer coverings for protection. The shells of armadillos, turtles, clams, and oysters, the quills of porcupines and hedgehogs, and the hard coverings of beetles help these animals protect themselves against enemies.

Plants also have protective coverings. Bark is the tough covering of trees. The pineapple protects the juicy fruit underneath with an outside covering that looks much like armor. Thirsty animals in the desert stay away from cactus plants because of their spines. The thorns of rose, raspberry, and blackberry bushes keep animals away. In what other ways do plants protect themselves?

Many animals are hidden from enemies by their coloring. Such coloring is called protective coloration. A polar bear, for example, is difficult to see against the white snow because of its white fur. Fish living near the surface of the water, and especially those swimming in the open sea, are steel-blue on the back. How does this coloring protect the fish? Is it easy to see a frog near a pond? Why?

Color hides many insects from their enemies. Grasshoppers may be as green as the grass and leaves

they feed upon. A twig-shaped insect, the walking stick, is green during the springtime when feeding upon young green plants. When the leaves fall in autumn, the color of the walking stick changes to a rusty brown. This color change hides the walking stick from its enemies. In the next activity, observe how hard it is to see a walking stick.

17/Observe

Put a walking stick in a jar with leaves and twigs. Let in air by punching several holes in the cover of the jar. Bring the jar to school. At first, your classmates may think you have only leaves and twigs in the jar. They will have to look carefully to see the walking stick. ■

Man has learned from nature to use color to hide objects he doesn't want seen. This is the art of camouflage (KAM-uh-flahzh). Buildings cannot be easily seen from an airplane when they are colored or covered to blend in with the surrounding scenery.

Some animals change color with the seasons, but others can change color in a few minutes. A flounder resting on a sandy ocean bottom will be evenly colored. If it swims to a place where there are stones and pebbles, the flounder will take on a spotted appearance that blends with the surroundings.

The ability to change color has made the American chameleon (kuh-MEE-lee-uhn) very well known. This little lizard will turn brown or green. The chameleon will change color according to temperature. These color changes are not sudden but take several minutes each

time to occur. Find out about blending coloring in the following activity.

18/Compare

Scatter three dozen toothpicks on a grassy area. Use 12 green, 12 red, and 12 white toothpicks. Each student can time himself as to how long it takes to find all the green toothpicks. Keep a chart of the numbers of each kind of colored toothpick found. Which were the easiest to find? Why? In what way does your finding more of one colored toothpick than another show how protective coloring works? ■

The toothpicks that were easiest to find did not blend with their background. It follows that those animals that blend in with their backgrounds are more difficult to see and can more easily escape their natural enemies.

Hornets, and other insects that sting, are usually yellow and black. Would you catch yellow and black insects in your bare hands? Why not?

The European fire-bellied toad produces certain substances from its skin which give it a bad taste. The toad has black markings on its legs and a bright red belly. When a stork or other bird flies down to catch the toad, it flops over on its back. The bright color warns the stork that this is a bad-tasting toad and it flies away.

Stripes on the back of a skunk are thought to be a fair warning of this animal's presence. The skunk's stripes are therefore called warning coloration. The skunk sprays its enemies with a bad-smelling liquid. How can you recognize a skunk?

59

Habits help animals protect themselves. American beavers cut down trees with their sharp teeth. The trees are used to build dams in ponds or streams. Mud, sticks, and stones are used to dam up part of a stream or river to form a pond. The beavers build their homes within the pond. These dams sometimes change the direction of water flow and cause flooding of surrounding land. Dams built by beavers may last for several years.

When faced with danger, some animals pretend to be dead. How would this pretense help an animal to escape its enemies? One animal in our country which is noted to pretend to be dead or hurt when an enemy approaches is the hog-nosed snake. The snake may hiss and attack. But it also may turn over on its back and pretend to be lifeless.

Some young birds, like the bobwhite, stay very still when their mother gives the signal that danger is near. This action is called "freezing". Until the mother bobwhite gives the baby birds the signal that all is clear, they remain "frozen". When she goes out into a field, the mother bird runs some distance from the nest before flying. You will not find the nest at the spot from which the mother bird flew. Why do you think she runs this distance before flying up?

TESTING YOUR IDEAS

Living things may have a tough covering, live in shells, be fast runners, have sharp teeth, or may be colored to blend with their surroundings. These features a) do not help living things in any way b) are helpful but not needed c) are necessary protection.

Different animals are protected from other living things differently in some ways. The kind of protection a living thing may have a) may be influenced by its surroundings b) may not be influenced by its surroundings.

HOW ARE ANIMALS AND PLANTS PREPARED FOR THE FUTURE?

Living things, prepared for winter, usually survive. The oak, elm, birch, and maple trees lose their leaves in the fall. The green of spring becomes the brown of winter, and the growth of plants stops. Beets and carrots have, however, stored food in their roots, and the white potato has an underground stem of stored food it can use to begin growth next spring.

The squirrel busily tucks nuts away in a hollow oak tree for his meals in the coming months. Gnawing mammals and man store up food for the winter. Beavers store pieces of bark and wood in the bottom of a pond so that they will have food even when the pond's surface and everything above ground are frozen. Squirrels, chipmunks, and beavers are busy in autumn storing food and preparing their homes for winter.

One half pint of wheat, a quart of hazel nuts, two quarts of buckwheat, and a few dozen acorns were the storehouse contents of one chipmunk. Holes are dug in the ground by squirrels for the nuts they eat during the winter. Some forget where they stored their nuts. How does this help the trees from which the nuts came?

Animals and plants, however, have a different kind of winter in their lives. This different winter is that all living things will someday die. What must happen to have animals and plants remain on earth? How have animals and plants adapted to a habitat in which living things die? The following investigation will help you answer this question.

19/Investigate

Obtain six lima beans. Notice the shape of the bean, that it is divided into halves, and that there is a small nub or bump on one side. Soak the beans in a glass of water overnight to loosen the halves and the bean's outer skin. On the following morning, remove the beans from the water. Hold one of the beans between your fingers with the nub of the bean face down on the table. Carefully separate the halves of the bean with a knife. Be sure that your teacher or an adult is present when you do this activity. What do you find between the halves of the lima bean seed? Do you find a new lima bean plant?

Now plant the remaining lima bean seeds in a container five inches deep filled with dark brown soil.

Plant the beans about an inch beneath the soil, and water the beans lightly every day. Wait a few days. What do you see growing in the container? Do you see new lima bean plants? ■

From the lima bean seeds grow new lima bean plants. In turn, these new plants will produce new seeds with new plants in them. By making new plants like the old which will in time die, plants are adapted to death.

Animals are adapted to death, for they can produce young, too. One day when the young are adults, they also will produce new animals of the same kind. What is the importance of seeds, new plants, and new animals? What would happen if animals and plants could produce young no longer? The making of new living things is the way animals and plants have adapted to surroundings in which all living things die.

The young must be cared for in some way. While most fish and water animals spend little time caring for their young, they lay many eggs in one season. One oyster may lay millions of eggs. Most of the eggs and many of the young oysters will be eaten by fish. But enough will grow into adults.

There are a few exceptions to the general rule that water animals do not care for their eggs and young. Male stickleback (STICK-ul-back) fish seem to plan carefully for their young. The male alone first builds an underwater nest. He brings in a female stickleback only when he has completed the nest. The female swims away after laying the eggs and doesn't return. The male moves his tail to keep a stream of fresh water flowing over the eggs. This water provides oxygen for the eggs. After six days, the eggs will hatch. The little fish are kept together by the male and protected until they are large enough to go off by themselves.

Whales and porpoises also take good care of their young. They give birth to live young. They do not lay eggs like most other swimming forms of life. Baby blue whales are 25 feet long at birth. The young whales gain about 200 pounds each day. Until the young whale is six or seven months old, its food is the milk of its mother. She protects her young from other animals during this period.

The mothers of lion and bear cubs protect and train them for almost two years. Five years is the length of time elephant babies stay close to their mothers. What is the name of the most helpless baby that comes into the world? If you say man, you are right! How many years does it take before a child can get along without parents? Think what would happen to you if you had to care for yourself without help from your mother and father.

TESTING YOUR IDEAS

All kinds of animals and plants must someday die. To preserve their kind on earth, living things must a) store food for the winter months b) protect themselves from all other living things at all times c) be able to have young.

ARE SOME KINDS OF ANIMALS AND PLANTS NO LONGER ON EARTH?

We know from a study of bones found in the earth that many millions of years ago there were huge reptiles called dinosaurs (DIE-no-sawrz) living on the earth. None is alive today.

We do not know all the reasons why the dinosaurs died out. Changing weather may have been one of them. The weather may have become too hot for the dinosaurs to live. As the great ice sheets covered areas of the earth, perhaps it became too cold for them

to get enough food. We know from our observations today, that weather has a very important effect on the lives of animals.

Many animals that cannot adapt to weather changes die every year. The hibernating turtle will freeze during the winter if it does not dig below the frost-line when making its winter home. Toads in hibernation will die if the land dries out. Floods and high water force rabbits and rattlesnakes from their burrows. What do you think happens to those that do not get out of their burrows? What happens to seeds that do not get enough moisture and soil? Find out in the next activity with weed and crop seeds.

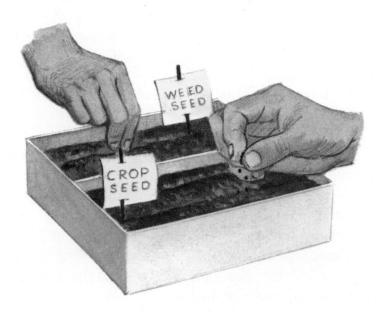

20/Observe

Some plant varieties may prevent the growth of others. Your teacher will give you the same number of weed seeds and crop seeds to plant in a pot or box.

Which seeds grow faster? Why do farmers have to get rid of weeds? ■

Weeds usually are strong plants. They take from the soil the nourishment needed by other plants. Weeds will take over an area if allowed to spread. Other plants and all animals will die if not given proper care and needed requirements. Relate this fact to the care of living things in a terrarium in the next activity.

21/Interpret

You have made a terrarium in your classroom or at home. If you have one, make a report on the plants and animals in it. If any of the animals or plants died, try to find out why. Did you have food and oxygen for the animals? Was there enough water for the plants? ■

Sometimes plants will appear to have all the things they need for good growth and still not do well. It has been found that some varieties of plants need specific minerals in the soil for them to do well. Without these minerals they do not reach their best growth. The use of proper fertilizers can often provide these missing minerals.

Plants and animals will die if they do not have the surroundings to which they are suited. If they are to survive, all the important needs must be fulfilled in their living and non-living environment.

Charles Darwin (1809-1882), a famous English scientist, once said that the amount of clover seed produced in one season depends on the number of cats living near the clover fields. This statement sounds strange until you listen to Darwin's reasoning.

Darwin

70

Cats eat the field mice which feed on bumblebees. The bumblebees help the clover so that it will produce seeds. When there are many bumble bees to help the clover plants, there is enough clover seed, and a large clover crop the next season. Clover hay is used by farmers to fatten their cattle.

These plant and animal relationships are called food chains or food webs. Think of another food chain and try to follow it as far back as you can.

Man stands at the top of many food chains. In the above example, how would the cost of meat be affected by an increase in clover hay?

Fish we eat are another good example of food chains. Man eats the big fish which eat the smaller ones. Little fish eat tiny water animals which feed on tiny water plants. Do you know where the tiny water plants get their food?

All animals were wild hundreds of thousands of years ago. They traveled over the earth searching for food and water. Later on, man began to tame some of these wild animals. The dog was probably the first animal to be tamed. Dogs may have been only companions at first. Man then found that these animals could help protect him.

Can you name some other kinds of domestic animals? What benefits does man receive from them?

Animals tamed by man supply him with many of the important things he needs. Animals helped man to do much of his work before the invention of modern machines. However, some of these animals are valued by man for their beauty or their amusing habits. The ancient Egyptians originally tamed the cat as a house pet. Anyone who has a pet monkey or has seen one enjoys their playful ways.

Man provides domestic animals with food and shelter in exchange for the benefits they give him. He cares for them if they become sick and protects them from their enemies. Most domestic animals have lived with man for such a long time that if allowed to run wild, they could not take care of themselves.

Domestic animals are only a small number of the different kinds of animals on the earth. Think of some of the wild animals that are highly valued by man.

Minks or foxes raised on ranches for their fur are not really tame. A ranch fox or mink would be able to survive in the wilderness.

The land was rich with forests, wild animals, fertile soil, and other natural resources when settlers first arrived in North America. These resources seemed so great that the American settlers believed that they would last forever. Forests were cut down to clear farmland and the wild animals were shot for food. The soil was often used unwisely and in time it became much less fertile. Great amounts of forest and grassland were destroyed by carelessly started fires.

Many wild animals were displaced from their natural habitats each time that man moved into a new area. Others were killed carelessly. For example, the American buffalo once roamed the plains in herds of many thousands. By the 1880's their total number became much smaller. Buffalo were often killed by the thousands, merely for the sport of the hunters.

The passenger pigeon was another North American animal that once was present in great numbers.

75

John James Audubon (1785-1851), the famous naturalist, reported in 1813 having seen a flock of passenger pigeons so huge it took three days for them to pass by. Not one passenger pigeon is alive today. They were all killed by hunters and changed conditions in their habitats.

Many people realized by the 1880's that the nation's resources were being used up rapidly by man's greed and carelessness. Such people wanted to stop the wasteful use of our resources. In order to protect our forest lands, wildlife, and other resources the conservation movement was started.

A powerful supporter of this movement was President Theodore Roosevelt. Help came from him to make conservation popular during his years as President (1901-1909). Many forest lands were put under government control, land for national parks was set aside, and hunting and fishing laws were passed. Are there any wild animals living near your area? Can they be hunted? Find out the legal seasons for fishing and hunting.

Animals and plants live in every kind of habitat, from the wettest to the driest, from the hottest to the coldest. It is not the same plants and animals that live and do well in these different climates. Each animal and plant lives in the place to which it is best suited.

Roosevelt

76

Man is very different from all the other animals. He alone can live almost anywhere on earth. Man can change his surroundings to suit him. Even though man cannot live without air to breathe, he doesn't have to stay where air is naturally present. Taking his atmosphere with him, man can travel under the ocean or far out into space. Clothing is made by man and he builds houses to protect him from the weather. He provides a comfortable climate in his house by heating or air-conditioning.

When man changes his surroundings to suit him, he must be careful not to ruin the land or harm the animals living on it. His responsibility is to use the natural world carefully so that it can be used and enjoyed by future generations. The more each individual learns about plants and animals, and about the ways they depend upon each other, the better he will be able to meet this responsibility.

TESTING YOUR IDEAS

With which of the following statements do you agree?

Changing weather conditions over a long, long period of time on earth have killed certain kinds of animals.

Changing weather conditions over a short period of time may kill some animals.

Man is the one animal who can directly change his environment.

Man can be a threat to animals and plants.

Below are listed particular statements about living things and general statements about living things. Which of the particular statements about living things are contained in each of the general statements? A general statement may explain more than one particular statement.

Particular Statement	*General Statement*

Particular Statement

1. The fur of the polar bear is white.
2. Milkweed seeds have "parachutes."
3. In spring, the ptarmigian looses its white feathers and grows brown ones.
4. Both a mountain and a flower pot are habitats.
5. Cactus grows in desert surroundings.
6. In winter, frogs hibernate.
7. Salmon swim to fresh water at certain seasons.
8. Some fish need warm water.

General Statement

A. A habitat is a place where living things live and grow.
B. Some animals change their habitat by migration.
C. The color of animals is influenced by their surroundings.
D. Dispersal occurs by chance.
E. Proper surroundings meet the needs of living things.
F. Some animals and plants have adapted to seasonal change.

A woodland terrarium was to be built by a science class. Dick and Barbara were chosen to build it. They knew living things need certain surroundings. But Dick grew tired of the idea of a terrarium.

"You know," he said to Barbara, "My uncle took me to a zoo yesterday. I saw zebras and elephants— all kinds of animals. They were all in the middle of the city, and all were brought from Africa. How come they can live here?" Barbara suggested animals perhaps could make a change.

"Do you mean adapt?" Dick asked.

How do you think animals from Africa can live in the city?

Find out how various seeds have been adapted so that they can travel from place to place. Collect play some of these seeds.

You are a State Forest Ranger. What plants and animals do you find in your region? What is the habitat of each? How can you protect these plants and animals?

You are a teacher planning to take your class on a field trip to study plants and animals. Where can you go? What will you see there? What plans should you make?

unit two
Your Growing Body

Have you ever wondered how the food you eat helps you to stay healthy and grow strong? Do you think that all kinds of foods in any amount are good for you? Do some foods make you healthier than others? Are some foods unhealthy to eat?

In the history of man, food has been a most important problem in different ways. You might imagine the first way food could be a great hardship — having enough to eat. During one period of the Roman Empire long ago, people chose to drown themselves rather than to starve. But even today some countries have very little food. Yet, is the amount of food you eat all that is important about food? Is it possible that to live and grow you need many different kinds of food in the right amounts?

For many years people knew very little about the way food helped them grow. They did not understand why some foods were better for them than others. They did not realize that a correct diet is needed to stay healthy and grow strong. Before people learned how to keep food from spoiling, they ate the food they could easily get. Meats and foods from grain could be had most of the year. But only in summertime were there plenty of fresh fruits and vegetables. At the times of year when people could not get much fresh food, they became easily tired or even sick. Children did not grow well. Some people died. In some countries at the present time, people may not be always hungry, but they are not healthy. They may have only a few kinds of food to eat, but to be well they need other kinds.

Today, many people may in some parts of the world overeat. If you eat too much, might you grow strong and healthy? Eating too much can be as great a problem as having too little food or not eating the right kinds.

Do you think a proper diet is necessary to live and grow strong?

WHAT FOODS DO YOU NEED?

Do you think there is something in fresh foods that helps you grow well and stay healthy? In this unit you will study about food and your growing body. In the first activity it might be fun for you to see how much you have grown.

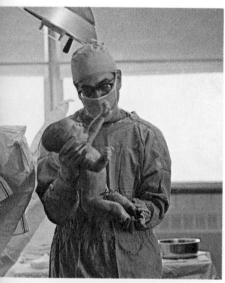

1/Compare

Bring to class a picture of yourself as a baby or as a small child. Also bring a recent picture of yourself. Put the pictures side by side to find out how you have changed. How much have you grown since the first picture was taken? How could you find out how much weight you have gained? What do you think helps you grow and keep healthy? ■

Imagine what would happen if there were no more food in the world. How would you feel if you did not have food every day? All the food you eat daily makes up your diet (DIE-uht). A diet that gives you the proper amounts of each food you need is called a balanced (BAL-unst) diet. One of the best ways to make sure you have a balanced diet is to plan your meals so that you eat the right kinds of food every day. What kinds of food do you think are needed in a balanced diet?

Look at the picture of a family eating a meal. What different foods are they eating? Do you see the meat, bread, butter, and vegetables? These are foods from four important food groups. The Milk Group includes milk, butter, cream, cheese, and ice cream. The Meat Group contains meat, fish, and poultry. The Bread Group includes bread, cereals, cakes, and pastries. The Vegetable Group is made up of vegetables and fruits.

The foods in these four groups contain the things which people need to be healthy and strong. Which two food groups come from animals? Which two come from plants? Do you know what most of the animals we use for food eat? Why can you call green plants the source of all food in the world?

2/Classify

Make up a page in your notebook for each of the four food groups. Look in magazines around your house to find pictures of different kinds of food. Cut out these pictures and paste them on different pages so that you have one page for each of the four food groups. Label each page according to its food group. ■

As you look at the pictures that you put in your notebook, you can see that many foods we eat belong to more than one food group. For example, a stew may be made from meat, fats, and vegetables. Or a cake may contain flour from wheat, butter, sugar, and milk. As you choose what to eat every day, you should have foods from each of the four main food groups.

The four main food groups are made up of many different foods. Each food may be made up of different materials. Because the different materials found in foods help us in different ways, we give them special names. You will learn more about these materials and their names as you do the activities in this part of your book.

For our bodies to have "go-power," we need a special kind of food. The "go-power" is called energy, and we need it for work and play. Its source is a special kind of food called a carbohydrate (cahr-bo-HIE-drayt). Sugars and starches are carbohydrates that we use every day. They are found in bread, cereals, potatoes, fruits, and, of course, sugar itself. Let us see if we can get some heat energy from sugar.

3/Describe

Put a piece of thin cardboard on top of any empty, clean tin can. Put a little pile of sugar in the middle of the cardboard. Have your teacher light the cardboard with a match so that it begins to burn and causes the sugar to burn also. After the burning sugar drops into the can, *carefully* touch the outside of the can. ■

Carbohydrates give us some of the energy that we need to live, grow, and work. When the weather is cold, do you think you need more or less carbohydrates? Do you use more energy when you work hard or when you are resting?

You can sometimes tell if sugar is found in a food by tasting it. It is not as easy to tell if starch is present. The following activity will help you discover which common foods contain starch.

4/Compare

Take a slice of raw potato, a piece of white bread, and a piece of cut apple. Put a drop of iodine on each of these foods. What happens to the color of the iodine on each piece? This change in the color of iodine on a particular food is a test for starch. Starch is one kind of carbohydrate. ■

Bring other foods to class and test them for starch, as before. In your notebook make a list like the one below of the foods that you tested and record your results.

Name of Food Tested	What Color Changes Take Place?	Does the Food Have Starch?
Potato	blue-black	Yes

Another kind of food we use is fat. As you learned earlier, a food substance that "burns" gives off energy. Let us find out if a fat or an oil is an energy food.

5/Observe

Your teacher will put a small amount of cooking oil or melted butter in a small dish. A thick string will

be dipped into the oil so that the string becomes soaked. Your teacher will then lift the end of the string up to form a wick and light it with a match. What do you see? Is fat or oil a good source of energy? ■

Which main food groups do you think are sources of fats or oils in your diet? Let us see how you can tell if a food has fat in it.

6/Compare

Rub a piece of butter or margarine on a piece of brown wrapping paper. Hold the paper up to the light and look at the spot on the paper. Now add a drop of water on the same piece of paper next to the grease spot. Hold the paper up to the light again and compare the two spots. What is the difference between the grease spot and the water spot after they dry? The spot left by the butter or margarine is a test for fats. Why is the water spot important? Test other foods for fats or oils. In your notebook make a list like the one below for the foods you test. ■

Name of Food Tested	Observations	Does it Have Fats?
Butter	grease spot	Yes

Fats are found in plants in the form of oils. Corn, soybeans, nuts, and olives are good sources of plant oils. We use animal fats in the form of lard, butter, and cream. Egg yolk, bacon, and cod-liver oil are also good sources of animal fat.

Your body uses carbohydrates and fats for energy. But while you are growing and working, different parts of your body, such as the muscles, skin, and glands, are slowly being worn out. To repair the worn-out parts, you must also have foods which contain proteins (PRO-teenz).

Meat, poultry, fish, eggs, and milk have all the proteins necessary for proper health and good growth. Vegetable foods, such as peas, beans, nuts, and cereal also contain proteins, but not enough to meet the protein needs of the body. From which group should you daily select food in order to supply the body with all the proteins it needs?

An easy way to test for proteins in food is to burn a small piece of the food and to notice how it smells. Let us try this test in the next activity.

7/Observe

Your teacher will hold a feather in a candle flame for a few seconds until the feather begins to burn. Note the way the feather smells when the flame is blown out. Watch your teacher hold a piece of lean meat in the flame with a pair of kitchen tongs. Compare its smell with that of the burning feather. Describe the smell. This is a test for proteins in food. ■

The foods you eat have carbohydrates and fats to provide energy, and proteins for repair and growth.

Another group of food substances you need is called minerals (MIN-ur-uhlz). Minerals help make your body healthy by building strong bones, hard teeth and healthy blood. Two common minerals are iron and copper, but, of course, you do not eat iron nails or chew pieces of copper wire! The minerals in the foods you eat are in forms that you can use. They are a part of many foods, but they are not even noticed. The table on page 93 shows you some of the common minerals that you require. Can you tell which food group is a good source of minerals?

Common Minerals in Foods

Mineral	Uses in Body	Food Sources
Calcium	Helps build strong bones and teeth; helps work of heart and muscles	Milk, cheese, beans, cauliflower
Copper	Helps work of blood; needed by tissues for growth	Liver, shrimp, bran, mushrooms, peas
Iodine	Used in controlling many activities of the body	Iodized table salt, sea foods
Iron	Used in blood to carry oxygen to tissues	Kidney meat, liver, spinach, whole wheat
Phosphorus	Helps form strong bones and teeth; used in tissues	Liver, beans, cheese, whole wheat, peas
Sodium	Helps in controlling body activities	Beef, table salt, bread
Sulfur	Used in making tissues in the body	Meat, fish, eggs, peas

The presence of different minerals in foods is hard to test. But the next activity will show you that foods contain minerals.

8/Observe

Put a small piece of bread or cheese in a plain metal dish, such as the lid from a jar. Your teacher will place the dish on a hot plate set on "high" or over a flame until all the food is burned up and the material in the dish stops smoking. The white or grayish ash in the bottom of the dish is made of minerals. What do you think has happened to all the other substances in the food? ■

You can see by looking at the table on page 93, that minerals are used for many purposes in the body. Although they are used in very small amounts, they help you to stay healthy and grow strong. By eating a balanced diet, you will have all the minerals you need.

Besides carbohydrates, fats, proteins, and minerals, another group of food materials you need is known as vitamins (VY-tuh-minz). These are found in many different foods and are needed, much like minerals, for you to stay healthy and grow strong. If a person does not have proper vitamins in his diet, he may develop certain diseases.

Many years ago sailors had little to eat during long trips besides dried meat and hard bread. They did not have fresh fruits or vegetables. The sailors often became ill with a disease called scurvy (SKUR-vee). This disease causes bleeding gums, loss of weight and a general feeling of weakness. Many sailors died because of scurvy. After many years it was discovered that eating oranges, lemons, and limes would prevent this disease. We now know that these and other fruits have a substance in them which we call Vitamin C.

In other parts of the world, some people liked to polish the brown covering off the rice that they ate. The people who ate such polished rice and little else very often became nervous and weak, lost weight, and could not work. When the rice was polished, something important was rubbed off. This something in the brown coat is what we call Vitamin B. Lack of Vitamin B in the diet causes a disease called beriberi (BER-ee-BER-ee).

The substances we call vitamins are usually named with letters of the alphabet. If you look at the label on most boxes of dry cereal, you will see the names of the minerals and vitamins found in these foods. As long as you eat a balanced diet, you will get all the minerals and vitamins necessary for good health.

One other material you need every day is water. Water does not directly supply materials to build or repair body parts, or to furnish energy. But you must have water to stay alive. Most of the body fluids, including blood, are made up of water. Water acts to dissolve food and waste materials and carry these materials to and from different parts of the body. Most of the water you need is gotten from drinking liquids, but many foods, such as fruits and vegetables, also supply water. Let us find out how much water some foods have.

9/Observe

Weigh a slice of freshly cut apple or potato carefully. Watch your teacher put the piece of food in a metal dish and warm it over a flame so that it becomes dry. The food should not be burned. Your teacher will heat it until there is no further loss of weight. Other foods can be tested in the same way. Use the headings below to make a table in your notebook. Write down the results of your tests. ■

Food Tested	Weight of Dish and Food Before Heating	Weight of Dish and Food After Heating	Weight of the Water Lost

Because water is so important to you in carrying on your life activities, you should drink plenty of water every day. Do you know how much water you lose from your body each day? Have you ever noticed how thirsty you get when you work hard and perspire a lot? You do not have to worry about drinking too much water. Every living thing uses what it needs and gets rid of the water it does not use.

TESTING YOUR IDEAS

Listed below are the four basic groups and some of the foods you may find in them. Try to plan a balanced menu for breakfast, lunch, and dinner. From the foods listed, it is possible to make other foods, such as a sandwich, stew, or cake. Not all the foods listed need be used, and you should add some of your own. An important substance we daily drink cannot be placed in any of the groups. Can you name it? Compare your menu with those of your classmates.

Meat Group	Milk Group	Bread Group	Vegetable Group
bacon	milk	flour	grapefruit
beef	cream	cereal (hot, cold)	potato
liver	butter (margarine)	rice	peas
fish	cheese	white, rye, or whole wheat bread	tomato
chicken	yogurt		string beans

98

WHAT HAPPENS
TO THE FOOD WE EAT?

Your body is growing. Inside your body are many parts which you cannot see. Each carries out a life activity for the body. They all work together to keep you living and growing. Each living thing whose parts act together as a unit is called an organism (OR-gan-izm). Some organisms have a few parts. Other organisms are much more complicated. The human organism, such as you, has many, many parts. For the parts to carry out their activities, they must be in good condition. Although your body has many parts all working at different jobs, you are one single organism. Those parts that work together to carry on one life activity form a body system (SIS-tem). Though you are one single organism, you have many systems. For example, the bones of your body form a strong movable framework. This framework gives your body the shape you see when you look in a mirror. The bones taken together are called the skeletal (SKEL-uh-t'l) system. Can you name some of the other systems in the body? If not, you will find out about them later.

Just as an organism like you is made up of systems, each system is made up of different parts, called organs (OAR-gunz). The stomach, for example, is an organ of the digestive system. Organs work together in helping the system do its job. In turn, each organ is made up of special materials called tissues (TISH-yooz). Your bones, your heart, and skin are each made of different types of tissue.

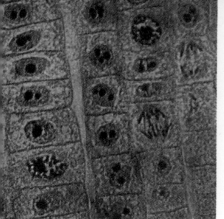

Onion cells magnified 600 times by a microscope magnified 60 times

10/Demonstrate

Peel off a piece of onion skin. Try to get the piece as thin as possible. Put this piece of onion skin on a moistened glass microscope slide. With your teacher's help, look at the piece of onion skin under a microscope or with a microprojector. Is the onion skin tissue one solid sheet, or is it made up of many parts? How are these tiny parts alike? How are they different? What can you see inside? ■

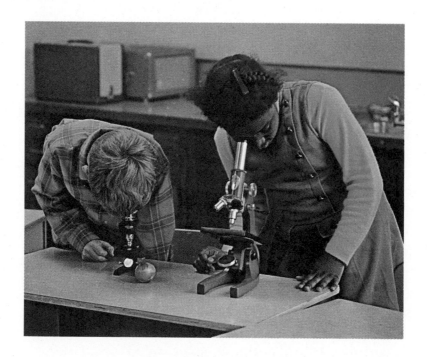

11/Observe

You can observe the tissue that forms the moist lining of your cheek. Your teacher will provide you with a clean tongue depressor and a glass slide. Using an eye dropper place a single drop of water on the

slide. Now, gently scrape the inside of your cheek with one end of the tongue depressor. Rub the wooden stick several times against the lining of your cheek and touch it to the water on the slide. Your slide is now ready, with your teacher's help, for study under a microscope or a microprojector. How does what you see compare with what you saw in the onion? Add a drop of iodine to your slide and observe the tissue again. What do you see this time? ■

All tissue is made up of many tiny units much like the ones you have seen. These units are called cells. They sometimes look as if they were bricks in a brick wall. But because your body is a unit, the cells are not like bricks; they work together in a very special way since you are one single organism. Cells are put together in a regular pattern in each different tissue. Your entire body is made up of millions and millions of cells which grow and multiply as you grow.

Can you guess what a cell needs to keep it alive? If you guess that it must have the food materials we learned about, then you are right. Cells use food. But an apple, a slice of roast beef or a piece of chocolate cake cannot be used by your body as they are. Quite a few changes must take place before it can be used by the cells. The activity in which food is broken down

Cells of cheek lining

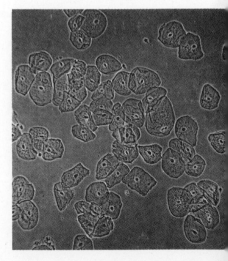

and dissolved so that it can be used by the cells is called digestion (die-JEST-shun).

Your cells use the materials in foods that are necessary for life. New cells grow. Energy for your growth comes from your food. To provide each cell the food that it needs in a form it can use is the job of the digestive system. The next activities will help you to understand more about digestion.

12/Explore

Put a piece of unsalted cracker or white bread in your mouth and chew it. Hold the chewed food in your mouth without swallowing it for a few minutes. Do you taste something different from the original taste? What does it taste like? Repeat the test with a piece of meat. Do you get the same results? ■

Digestion begins in the mouth. As soon as food is put into the mouth, the food begins to change. When you chew a bite of white bread, what changes do you notice?

The moisture in your mouth, called saliva (suh-LIE-vuh), wets the food as you chew it and begins to change it. Starch is found in bread and is changed by the saliva into a kind of sugar.

Your tongue is very important in tasting and chewing food. The tongue moves the food around in the mouth as it is chewed, so that the teeth can crush and grind the food. After the food is chewed well, the tongue pushes the food to the back of the mouth so the food can be swallowed. The next time you eat, pay attention to the movements of your tongue from the time food is put into your mouth until the food is swallowed. Do you think it makes a difference whether food is chewed well or not? Do the next activity to see if you can find out.

13/Compare

Cut a peeled, raw potato into three pieces of the same size. Partly fill three jars with water. Put one piece of potato in the first jar. Cut the second piece of potato into 15 or 20 pieces and put them into the second jar. Rub the third piece of potato on a grater to make the pieces very fine. Put these pieces into the third jar.

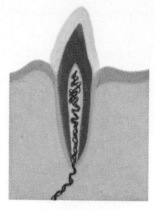

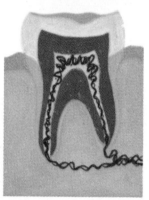

Now, put the lids on the jars and shake each jar for a few minutes. Remove all the pieces of potato from the water, using a strainer if necessary. Now add 10 drops of iodine to each jar and compare the color of the liquid. Describe any differences you see in the depth of color in three jars. Which of the jars showed that more starch was released? What does this activity show you about chewing your food well? ■

You need strong teeth to chew your food properly. Therefore, you can see why you should take care of your teeth and brush them well. Teeth are hard and much like bones, but a tooth that is broken or has a cavity in it will not grow together as a bone will. Teeth are covered with the hardest material found in the body. Even this hard material depends on the food you eat.

Everyone has two sets of teeth during his life. We call the first set the baby teeth, and there are 20 of these. Do you still have some of your baby teeth? We

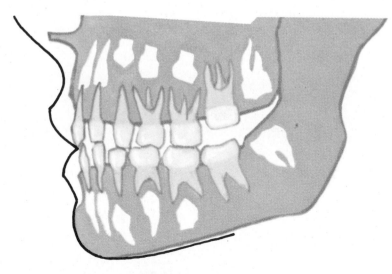

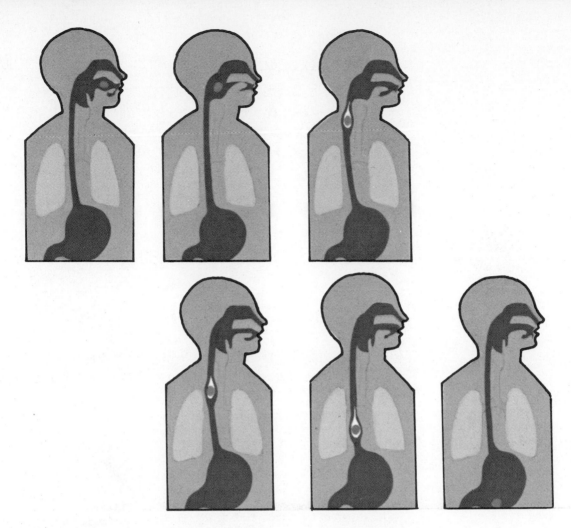

call the second set the permanent teeth. As the teeth of your second set begin to grow, they push against the baby teeth causing them to loosen and come out. Most people will have 32 permanent teeth when they grow up.

Chewed food is swallowed by passing through a long muscular tube leading to the stomach. Liquids pass very quickly through this tube. The chewed foods are moved down to the stomach by a special wave-like action of muscles which make up the tube. You can see how this action takes place by doing the next activity.

14/Illustrate

Put a marble in a rubber tube. Squeeze the tube to make the marble move through it. The marble moves somewhat like the way food moves through the tube that leads to the stomach. ■

To get the food into other organs where it will be changed even more than in the mouth, the muscles in front of the food relax, while the muscles behind the food contract. Thus, the food is squeezed along. This wavelike action of the muscles allows you to swallow even though your head may be lower than your stomach. In animals with long necks, such as giraffes or swans, food often moves first downward then upward to the stomach.

The food, as it moves along, enters the stomach (STUM-uck). The stomach does not grind up food the way the mouth does. But in the stomach food is mixed with juices from special organs that help in digestion. These digestive juices begin to break down foods. The churning action of the stomach, together with the way the digestive juices act on food, changes

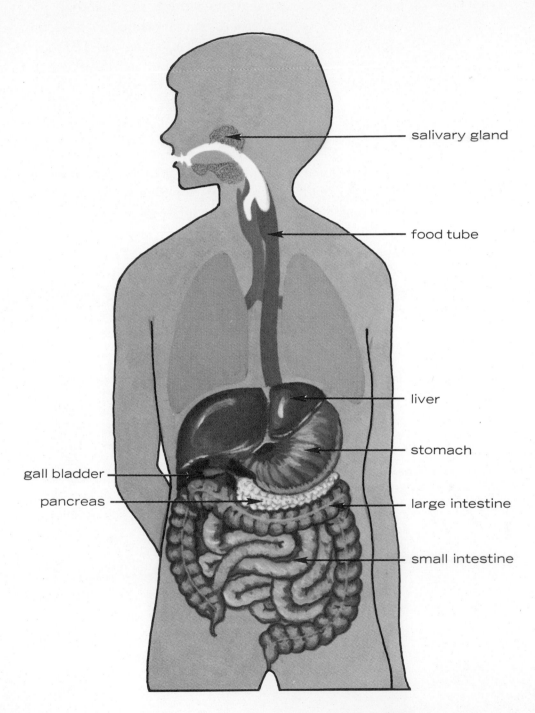

salivary gland

food tube

liver

stomach

gall bladder

pancreas

large intestine

small intestine

most of the food we eat into a thick, soft material. This thick liquid material leaves the stomach and goes into another organ called the small intestine (in-TESS-tin) where more changes take place. Let us see if we can find out how these changes take place.

15/Observe

Boil some lean meat until it is tender. Cut the meat into small pieces about 1/4 inch square. Fill two small jars half-full of water and put a few pieces of meat in each one. Add a pinch of meat tenderizer to one jar and put the lids on both jars. Place the jars in a warm place overnight. Compare the liquid in the two jars the next day. Describe what you observe. ■

The changes you see are caused by a digestive material which is sold as a meat tenderizer. Your body produces a number of these digestive materials which act very much like meat tenderizer. Juices containing the digestive materials are made in the body by special organs called glands (GLANDZ). There are digestive glands in the mouth, in the stomach, and in the small intestine. There are digestive juices that help break down carbohydrates, fats, and proteins. Do the next activity to find out more about digestion.

16/Observe

Watch your teacher boil about a cup of water and add a level teaspoon of starch. The mixture should be stirred until the starch dissolves and forms a cloudy mixture. To one test tube add a teaspoon of saliva to the mixture. To the other test tube add a teaspoon of water. Shake the test tubes and put them in a pan of warm water for ten minutes. Now add a few drops of Benedict's solution to each test tube. Your teacher should heat the water to boiling. Note what happens to the color of the liquid in each test tube. Describe what happens. This color change shows that simple sugar is present. Did you find sugar in both test tubes? Explain your answer. ■

Saliva is a digestive juice produced by glands in the mouth. Does the thought of a nice, juicy hamburger make your mouth water? If this happens, the digestive glands are getting ready to digest food that you might eat. The smell of food cooking, or the sight of food when you are hungry makes the glands begin producing digestive juices.

The liquid food that passes from the stomach into the small intestine mixes with digestive juices produced by glands in and outside the small intestine. The glands outside the intestine are the liver (LIV-uhr) and pancreas (PAN-kree-uhs). Their digestive juices complete the digestion of carbohydrates, fats, and proteins.

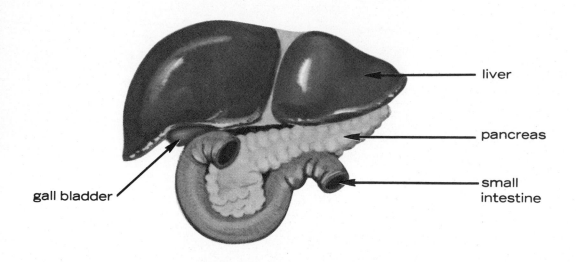

gall bladder

liver

pancreas

small intestine

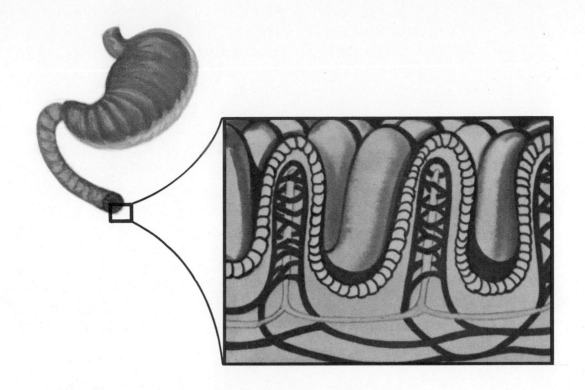

The breakup of food in the small intestine is the last step in digestion. As the wavelike action of the muscles continues to move the food along, tiny blood vessels in the walls of the intestine take in the digested food. The food you eat becomes part of your blood. The digested food is now in a form that the cells can use as it is carried along with the blood. How can the food pass through the walls of the intestine? Let us see if we can find out.

17/Explain

Carefully crack the shell on the large end of a fresh egg and peel away some of the shell. Do not break the thin "skin" just under the shell. Take a small glass

jar in which the egg will fit without touching the bottom and fill the jar with water until it comes halfway up the side of the egg.

At the other end of the egg make a small pinhole through the shell and "skin." Fasten a short piece of clear plastic straw over the hole with modeling clay so that the seal is airtight. Put the peeled end of the egg in the water. Observe the straw every 15 minutes. Keep a record of your observations. Can you explain what happens? You have made a model that shows something about the way digested food passes into the cells of your body. In what form would food have to be in order to pass through the "skin" of your cells? ■

You may wonder why we call the small intestine "small" when it seems to occupy so much of the body. It is called small, not because it is short but because it is narrower than the large intestine. The large intestine is wider than the small intestine, but it is also shorter.

The main part of digestion is completed within the small intestine. The soft, wet material that passes into the large intestine is made up mostly of things that the body cannot digest. In the large intestine water is taken back into the blood stream so that only soft, solid wastes are left.

The wavelike action of the muscles moves the solid wastes slowly along the large intestine. The wastes finally reach the end of the digestive system. The large intestine has an opening at its end to the outside of the body, and the undigestable wastes are passed out through this opening.

Think of all that happens in your body after you eat!

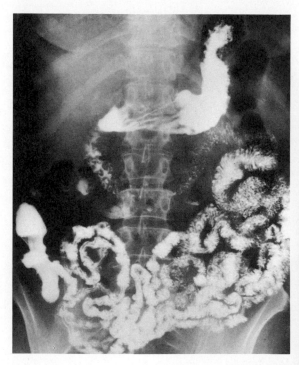

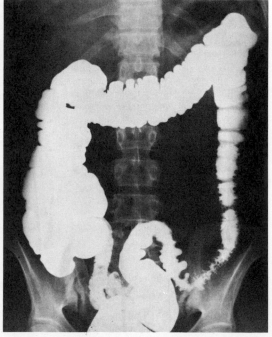

Which of the following lists shows the order of the parts of the digestive system?

mouth	mouth	mouth	food tube
food tube	stomach	food tube	mouth
stomach	food tube	stomach	stomach
large in-testine	small in-testine	small in-testine	small in-testine
small in-testine	large in-testine	large in-testine	large in-testine

With which of the following statements do you agree?

Two of the most important glands of the digestive system are the pancreas and the stomach.

All foods may be directly used by the body.

All parts of the foods we eat are completely digestible.

WHAT HAPPENS TO DIGESTED FOODS?

The digestive system has the job of breaking apart solid food and changing it into liquid so that it may be used by all of your cells. How do you suppose the digested food gets from the tube where it is digested to the cells of your fingers, toes, arms, and legs? How do you think the liquid food gets to every part of your body? The system that gets food to all parts of your body is made up of tubes, a hollow pump, and blood. Food materials enter the blood by passing through both the cells of the small intestine and the cells that make up the smallest blood tubes.

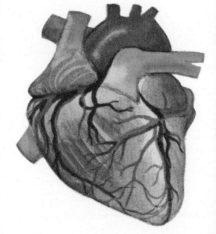

Blood is pumped to all parts of the body by the action of the heart. The heart pumps blood by contracting its muscles. The heart is a powerful muscle with four parts through which the blood flows. Each time the heart beats, the muscles contract and about one-fifth of a cup of blood is pumped to your body.

To find where the heart is located in your body, let us do the next activity.

18/Locate

Make a loose fist with your left hand. Place it over the center of your chest and pull your fist slightly to the left. Point your thumb toward your right shoulder to make sure your fist is in the right position. This is about the location of the heart inside your chest. Now

place a cardboard tube against the chest of another student and put your ear to the tube. What do you hear? Can you hear the other student's heart beating? Is it beating at a steady rate? What is happening to the blood each time you hear a beat? ■

The main job of the heart is to act as a pump which keeps the blood moving through the body. If you listen carefully, you can hear a "lub" sound and a "dup" sound in each beat. These sounds are caused by the opening and closing of folds of tissue that act as one-way doors in the heart. The one-way doors called valves (VALVZ) serve to keep the blood flowing in one direction. The speed of this pumping action depends on your body activity.

The heart pumps blood to the lungs where it takes in oxygen from the air you inhale. The blood then returns to the heart. Next, the blood goes out to all other parts of the body. It picks up digested food from the small intestine and takes it to the cells of the body. The blood also picks up liquid waste which it carries to the organs that dispose of it.

How is the heart able to do all these things? Look at the picture of the heart on this page. You can see four "rooms" in which the blood collects. Facing another student, you can think of his heart as having a right side (to your left) and a left side (to your right).

As the heart begins its beat, the blood moves through the valves from the top rooms into the bottom rooms. Then as the beat continues, the blood moves out of the lower rooms into blood tubes that carry it to all other parts of the body. When the heart relaxes at the end of its beat, some blood comes back into the room on the upper right side of the heart. This blood collects from the body parts. At the same time, blood collects in the upper left room as it comes from the lungs. Then, on the next beat, the action is the same

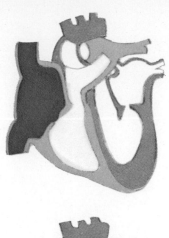

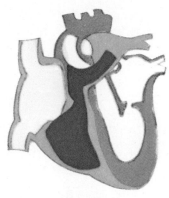

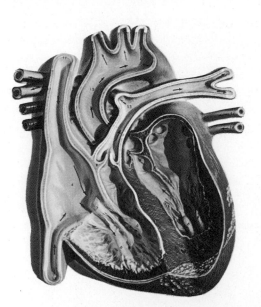

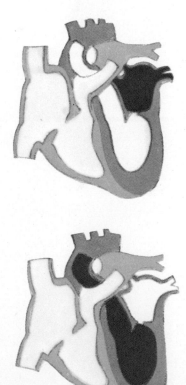

again. Do you know how fast your heart beats? You can find out in the following activity.

19/Count

Let your hand bend forward a little at the wrist. Press the first two fingers of your other hand into the little hollow spot under the wrist just in back of the thumb, as shown in the picture. Sit quietly so that you can feel something pushing up against your fingers. This repeated pushing and throbbing is something called a pulse. You can feel your pulse beating. When your teacher says, "Start," begin counting to yourself the number of times you feel a push against your fingers. When the teacher says, "Stop," stop counting and write down the number of beats you counted in your pulse. Repeat this several times. How many times does your heart beat in one minute when you are sitting

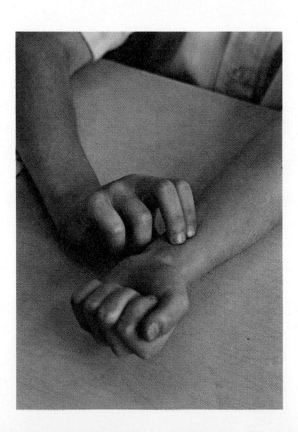

quietly? How many times does your heart beat after
you do some exercise? ■

Every time your heart muscles contract, blood is
pumped out into the blood tubes. This contraction of
the heart muscles is your heartbeat. At certain points
in your body you can feel the repeated push of blood
through your body. Does it take some time for the
blood to move to different parts of the body? Let us
see if we can find out?

20/Compare

Locate the beating of the pulse in your neck (under the hinge of the jawbone alongside the windpipe).
Now locate the pulse in the blood vessel on the inside
of the ankle (just behind the knob of the ankle bone).
Place your middle finger on the pulse in the neck and
the middle finger of your other hand on the pulse in
the ankle. Sit quietly for a minute and note what happens. What difference do you find in these two points
where you feel the pulse? ■

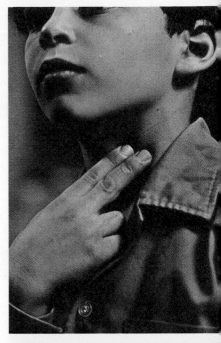

Your heart pumps blood to all parts of the body,
the head, the arms, the intestines, and the lungs. Your
heart also pumps blood to itself by means of small
blood tubes that are located in the heart muscles themselves.

As your heart pumps, many changes take place in
the blood. To find out more about these changes let
us suppose that we can follow one drop of blood as it
makes a trip through the body.

The blood has to travel along two main routes. It
goes to the lungs to pick up oxygen and release waste
gases that are breathed out. It also carries this oxygen

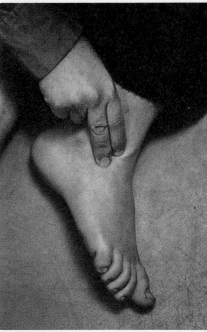

119

together with digested food from the small intestines to other parts of the body.

Let's trace a drop of blood as it moves through your body. Look at the drawing to help you trace the drop. As a drop of blood leaves the heart, it goes out

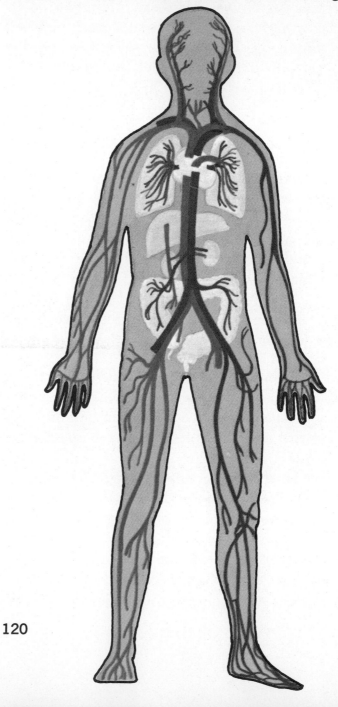

into a large blood tube that carries blood away from the heart. All tubes carrying blood *away from* the heart are called arteries (AR-tur-ees). The large artery leading out of the heart branches into a tube that leads to the head and another that leads to the lower parts of the body. These smaller arteries branch even more, becoming smaller and smaller in size. After the artery has branched many times, the tiny blood tubes are called capillaries (KAP-i-ler-eez). At this point, the drop of blood passes through a tissue in the body. Here it gives up to the body cells the digested food materials which it has picked up from the small intestine. The blood also gives up the oxygen which it has picked up from the lungs. At the same time, the blood takes up any wastes which are in the tissue and need to be carried away.

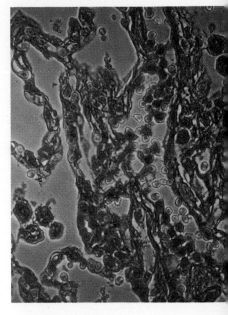

Microscopic view of blood cells in capillaries

On the way back to the heart, the drop of blood goes into larger and larger blood tubes. All blood tubes returning blood *to* the heart are called veins (VAYNZ). The drop of blood moves into one of the big veins that carries blood into the heart. Once here, the journey of each drop of blood begins all over again. The drop of blood leaves the heart by way of an artery that leads to the lungs. Here it picks up oxygen and releases the waste gases you breathe out. The blood finally comes back to the heart by way of veins for another trip around the body.

What happens to one drop of blood will happen to all of the blood. Your body has a very organized system of hollow tubes to get blood from place to place. You can imagine how important it is to have a healthy heart pumping blood through your body every second of your life. Blood is important and necessary for your life because it helps keep all of your body's cells alive. What is blood made of?

Healthy blood cells seen through a microscope

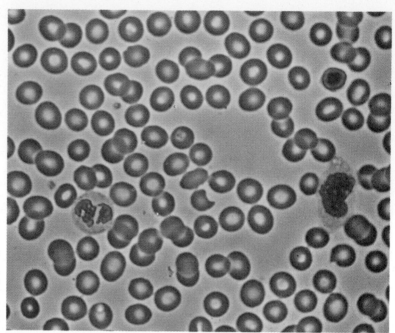

Microscopic view of red blood cells

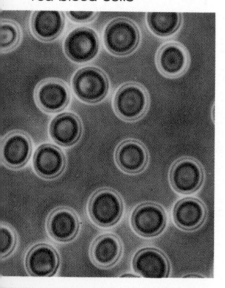

Microscopic view of white blood cells

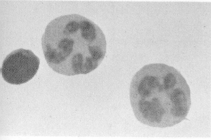

Look at the picture on this page which shows a sample of blood as you would see it under a microscope. The little cells you see give blood its color. Although each cell is not very red, blood is red in color. Do you know why it is red?

Blood can be thought of as being made up of two parts. The liquid part, or plasma (PLAZ-muh) carries digested food and waste materials. The solid part is made up of cells. Some cells pick up oxygen in the lungs and carry it to the different parts of the body. These are called red cells. Other blood cells, the white cells, attack germs that get into the body and fight infections.

Your growing body makes the materials that form your blood from the food and water in a balanced diet. Try to remember the first step to proper health. Eat the right kinds of foods.

With which of the following statements do you agree?

The system of the heart, blood tubes, and blood does not depend upon the digestive system.

The digestive system does not depend upon the system of the heart and blood tubes.

The system of capillaries is spread throughout the body, because no matter where you are cut you will bleed.

If the system of capillaries is spread throughout the body, then arteries and veins are spread throughout the body too.

Blood tubes which go away from the heart are arteries and carry oxygen and food. Blood tubes that go to the heart are veins and carry wastes. But is the blood tube going from the lungs to the heart an artery or vein? Remember, it carries oxygen. Is the blood tube going from the heart to the lungs an artery or vein? Remember, it carries wastes.

WHAT HAPPENS
WHEN FOOD AND OXYGEN COMBINE?

Have you ever run across the playground and up the stairs? In goes one breath, and out goes another. What do you think is going in and out of your body so fast? If you say it is air, you are right! The most important substance for us in air is oxygen (AHKS-i-jin). We need this substance to stay alive. The air you breathe is made up of several gases, one of which is oxygen.

As you breathe, the air follows a special pathway into the body. Look at the drawing on page 125. With your finger, follow the arrows from the nose to the lungs. The system by which you breathe in oxygen and breathe out other gases is called the respiratory (RES-puh-ruh-taw-ree) system. Can you name some of the organs making up the respiratory system?

Open your mouth and look in a mirror. Can you see a red, moist lining in your mouth? The organs of the respiratory system also have a very thin, moist lining. This kind of tissue has many tiny blood vessels in it. It is always wet, and dry air passing through the nose is warmed and moistened by this lining.

Inside the nostrils of your nose are tiny hairs which catch small particles of dirt and prevent the dust from passing into your lungs.

You can see why it is important that the air passages of your nose be kept open and clean. Air has to be able to go through them easily, and your nose has an important purpose. It warms, cleans, and moistens the air as it goes into your body.

124

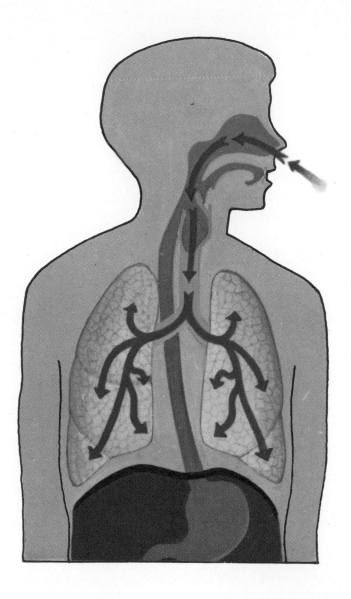

When you have a cold, the moist lining in your nose swells up. The air passages fill with fluids, and you cannot breathe through your nose. Think of your mouth as an extra safety passage for air to be used only when your nose cannot do its job.

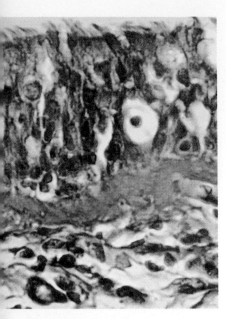

Windpipe tissue with hairlike threads. Magnified 250 times

As you can see in the drawing on page 125, an organ called the windpipe connects the back of the nose and mouth with the lungs. The windpipe is lined with the same kind of tissue as the nose. The lining in the windpipe also has very tiny, hairlike threads which move back and forth and remove dust and germs from the air we breathe in.

Has soap powder or pepper ever made you sneeze? Your body has another way to keep dust and other fine particles out of the respiratory system. If something gets into the air passages which might be dangerous, you cough or sneeze until it is removed.

Look at the drawing of the respiratory system again. Notice how the windpipe branches into two tubes. One goes to the left lung and the other goes to the right lung. The lungs, which are made up of very spongy tissue, are at the ends of these air tubes. The lungs take up most of the space inside the chest. Inside

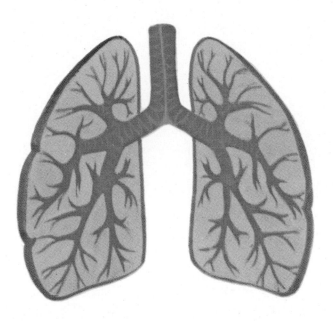

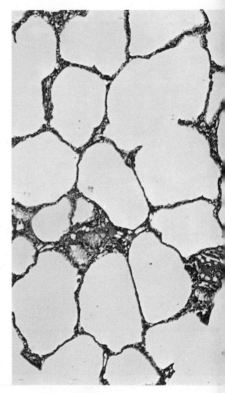

Air sacs of lung magnified 250 times

the lungs, the air tubes divide into smaller and smaller tubes. At the ends of each of these tiny tubes are very tiny, balloon-like parts called air sacs.

These little "balloons" or air sacs are so tiny that you can see them only with a microscope. The drawing on **this** page shows you what they might look like. They look like little bunches of grapes. These tiny, hollow sacs make up the spongy tissue of the lungs. Each air sac is surrounded with tiny blood capillaries.

As you breathe in, air goes into the little sacs. Oxygen from the air passes through the thin walls of the air sacs into the blood. At the same time, waste products that are in the blood pass into the air sacs so that the waste can be removed from the body when you breathe out.

As you know, the oxygen taken up by the blood is carried to the tissues of the body. Do you remember what part of the blood carries oxygen? Do you remember what was produced when sugar burned? You will become familiar with burning and its products in the next unit. But when sugar burned, what did you see and feel? The oxygen combines with the carbohydrates in the cells in somewhat the same way that sugar combines with oxygen. As the food and oxygen are used by the cells, waste products are formed and energy is given off. Do you know the names of the main waste products formed when carbohydrates and oxygen are used in the body? Let us see if we can find out in the following activity.

21/Explain

Dissolve a level tablespoon of sugar in a glass of warm water. Sprinkle a little powdered yeast into the water and stir. Fill a clean pop bottle half-full with this liquid. Put a plastic or rubber tube into the bottle so that the end of the tube is above the liquid. Seal the opening of the bottle around the tube with modeling clay, as shown in the picture . Put the other end of the tube in a glass of limewater. After a few minutes,

what do you see coming out of the end of the tube in the glass? What happens to the color of the limewater? Do you know what gas this is a test for? Where does the gas come from? ■

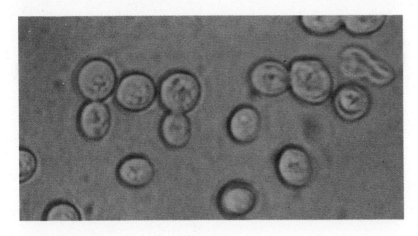

Yeast cells magnified 600 times

The yeast is made up of tiny cells which are in a resting state. When the yeast is added to warm water and sugar, the cells begin to grow and divide. To do this they must have energy. Do you know what these cells use for energy? If you say the sugar, you are only partly right! The cells also take in oxygen from the air and combine it with the sugar to get energy to grow and divide. When this happens, a waste gas is produced. You see it bubbling out of the tube into the glass of limewater. The name of this gas is carbon dioxide. It is also formed by the cells in your body, and you breathe it out in the air leaving your lungs.

Take a deep breath and hold it for about 30 seconds. Slowly let it out. What happens to your chest when you breathe in? What happens when you breathe out? Can you explain how air is able to enter your lungs when you breathe in? Let us do the next activity to see if we can find out.

22/Demonstrate

Fit the glass chimney of an old-fashioned lamp with a rubber balloon and a piece of rubber sheeting, as shown in the drawing. Pull down on the rubber sheeting and note what happens to the balloon. How does this activity show how the air goes in and out of your lungs? ■

Air is moved in and out of the lungs as the chest expands and contracts. Directly under the ribs is a large muscle, called the diaphragm (DIE-uh-fram), which controls breathing. When the diaphragm is relaxed as you breathe out, it fits up under the ribs and fills the space at the bottom of the chest cavity. When you breathe in, the diaphragm tightens and flattens along the bottom of the chest cavity, making more room for the lungs to fill with air. In the activity you just did, what part of the model acts like the diaphragm?

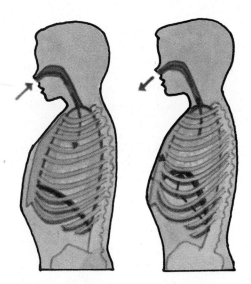

How fast does the in and out breathing take place in your body? Let us do the next activity and see how many times a minute you breathe.

23/Record

Everyone in the class should sit quietly for this activity. Look at a classmate and count the number of times his chest rises and falls. When the teacher says "Start," begin to count the number of times the person breathes. When the teacher says "Stop," stop counting and write down the number of times the person breathed. Compare your count with the counts your classmates made. Your teacher will help you figure out the average number of breaths per student. ■

The blood carries digested foods, water and oxygen to the cells where they are used. As the cells use the materials for repair and growth or to release energy, they produce materials which they cannot use. These are called waste products and must be removed from the body if it is to stay healthy. The blood picks up these waste materials and carries them to special organs which remove them from the blood. The system that gets rid of body wastes is made up of the lungs, the skin, the kidneys, and the bladder. As you can see, an organ may do more than one thing in the body. Do you now see why the living human body is not like a wall of bricks laid together? What two things are done by your lungs?

The lungs are important in getting rid of waste products, as well as in supplying oxygen to the body. Do you know what two waste products are given off by the lungs? Do the next activity to see if you can find out.

24/Test

Breathe onto the cool surface of a mirror or a glass. What forms on the surface? Where does this material come from? Use a clean drinking straw to blow your breath gently through a glass of limewater. What happens to the color of the limewater? What gas must be given off? Now you can name the two waste products that are given off by the lungs. ■

The two waste products found in the air we breathe out are made by the cells when the cells use carbohydrates to supply energy for the body. Other parts of the body get rid of wastes produced when cells are repaired or destroyed. These parts are the two kidneys, the bladder and the tubes that lead from the kidneys to the bladder to the outside of your body.

Look at the drawing on this page. Find the kidneys which are located at the back of the body cavity, a few inches above the waist. Below the kidneys, at the very bottom of the body cavity, is the hollow, muscular bag called the bladder.

Waste materials are collected from the cells of the body by the blood. The blood goes through the kidneys where the liquid waste materials are removed. These then go into the bladder where they are stored. When the bladder fills up, you become aware that liquid waste must be removed from the body.

Although we think of the skin as a covering tissue of the body, it also helps the body get rid of waste materials. Do you remember what happens to the skin of your face and hands when you work in the hot sun? This liquid is formed by the sweat glands in the skin. It is a waste product made up mostly of water with some salts in it. Let us take a closer look at the skin.

25/Observe

Use a magnifier to look at the skin on the back of your hand. Using a mirror, look at the skin on your face. These are the pores through which sweat leaves

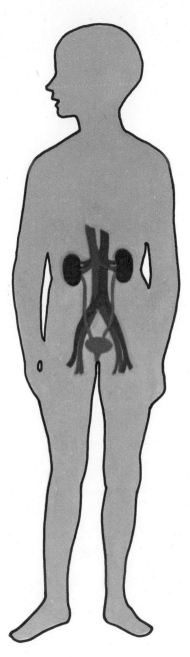

133

the body. Rub your finger alongside your nose. Do you feel an oily substance? This oil is produced by oil glands in the skin. Can you guess why we need this oil on our skin? ■

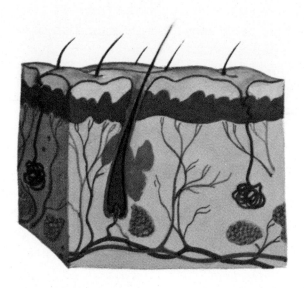

Look at a magnified drawing of the skin on this page. As you can see, the skin is more than just a layer on the outside of the body. The skin gets rid of water and salts by way of sweat. It also helps the body control its temperature. As sweat evaporates from the skin, it cools the body. Can you explain why you sweat a lot when you are exercising?

Because the skin is an important part of your waste removing system, care of the skin is important for good health. If your skin is not properly cared for, the pores may become clogged. Such clogging will prevent the pores from getting rid of wastes. What do you think could happen if the oil glands become filled up with dirt? It is a good habit to bathe yourself with warm water and soap every day.

With which of the following statements do you agree?

The production of energy in the body makes wastes.

The kidneys are not the only means by which the body rids itself of wastes.

The respiratory system, the digestive system, and the system of the heart and tubes have nothing in common at all.

Which is the correct order a particle of oxygen might follow in the respiratory system?

nose	nose	nose
windpipe	air sacs	windpipe
air sacs	windpipe	air tubes
blood	air tubes	air sacs
air tubes	blood	blood

HOW DOES YOUR BODY MOVE?

The food you eat is digested in your body and is carried to all of your cells by the blood. Oxygen in the tissues combines with the food, and energy is released in the cells. What do you think happens to this energy in the body? If you say, "To do all the things we do," you are right. But you may not know the body is able to perform all these actions.

One of the main things you do is to move around. You walk, you run, you write, you comb your hair, and you do many other things every day. How are you able to do all these things?

26/Observe

With your right hand, hold the tip of a finger on your left hand. Squeeze slightly along the sides of the finger, moving your hand up to the wrist, forearm, elbow, upper arm, and shoulder. Do you feel the bones in your hand and arm? Can you feel the different types of bones? ■

Bones form the framework of your body. This system supports the body and gives it the shape you see and feel.

When you were born, your skeleton was not as hard and strong as it is now. Much of it was made of a rubbery tissue called cartilage (KAR-ti-lij). As you grow, most of the cartilage is changed to bone tissue.

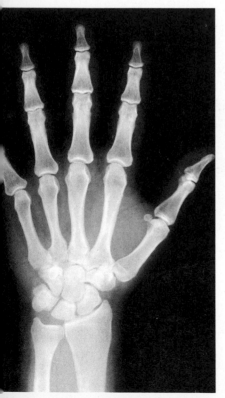

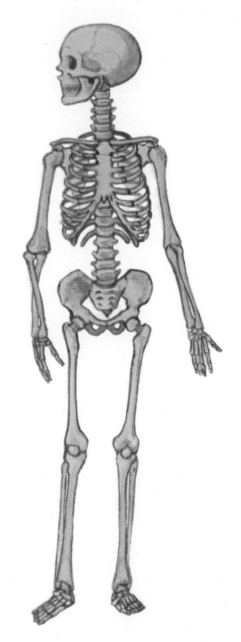

By the time you are fully grown, your body will have
206 bones making up your skeleton. Look at the drawing of the skeleton on this page. Can you find and
name some of the main parts of the skeleton?

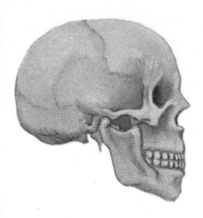

Slide your hand from your forehead across the top of your head and feel the sides of your head. What part of the skeleton do you feel? Move your fingers up and down along the sides of your chest. What bones do you feel there? Feel the large, flat bone in front of your chest. Find the collarbones on each side and on top of the chest. Can you feel two large, flat bones in the upper part of your back? ■

You have been studying where many of the organs of the body are found. Do you remember where the heart and lungs are in the body? What parts of your body are found near the collarbones, breastbone,

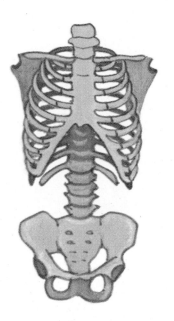

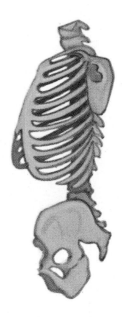

ribs, and shoulder blades? Are these parts inside or outside of the chest? Can you see any reason why the bones of the skull are all around the brain? If you have figured out that these bones help keep your heart, lungs, and brain from being hurt, you have the answers to these questions. An important use of the skeleton is to protect other organs in your body.

Move your arms back and forth. Put your hand on the back of your neck and move your head. Bend over and touch the floor. You are able to do all these things in part because of your skeleton.

In order to be able to move, the bones fit together at places in the skeleton which we call joints (JOYNTS). You have different kinds of joints in your body. See if you can find out which kind of movement each joint can do.

139

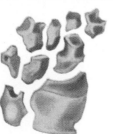
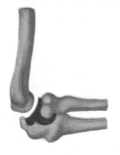
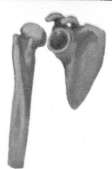

28/Describe

Place your arm on the desk so that the palm is up. Hold your wrist with the other hand and turn your arm over so that the palm is down. Describe what kind of motion you feel in the two bones of the arm.

Hold your arm straight out and put your other hand on the bottom of the elbow. Bend the arm back and forth. What kind of motion do you feel in this kind of joint?

Put your hand on the opposite shoulder of your body. Swing your arm around. What kind of motion do you feel in the shoulder joint? ■

140

Of course, the bones in your body do not move by themselves. You have muscles. The muscles of your muscular (MUS-kyoo-lur) system make the bones move. You can control many of your muscles. You can move when you want to and stop when you want to. Look at the drawings on this page to see where most of these muscles are found.

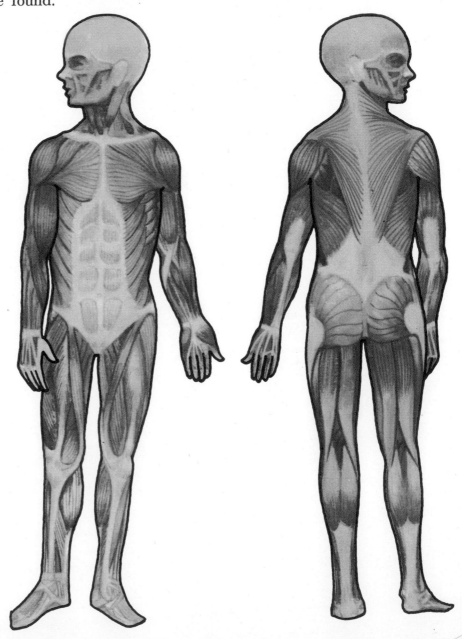

There are other muscles in the body that you do not have to think about to make them move. Do you have to think about moving the diaphragm in order to breathe? Can you name other muscles that move without your thinking about them?

Muscles must have energy to move. Now do you understand why you must have energy foods in your diet? The carbohydrates you eat are digested into forms that can be carried by the blood and taken in by the cells. There oxygen changes the digested food into other materials, and small amounts of energy are given off. Every time you take a step, bend your finger, or take a breath, muscle cells are using some of this energy. Do you remember what else is formed in the body when food materials are used? Energy is needed by all of the muscle cells of the body. Let us see how some of your muscles work.

Cells of muscle tissue magnified 800 times

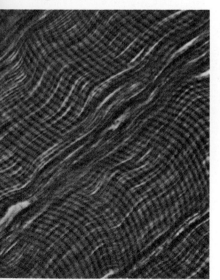

29/Observe

Feel the muscles of your upper arm. When the muscle on the front of the upper arm contracts, it becomes shorter and fatter. What happens to the forearm when this muscle contracts? Feel the muscle over the back part of your upper arm. What happens to the forearm when this muscle contracts? Can you find other muscles in your body which work in pairs like these two muscles? ■

The drawing on page 143 shows you how these two muscles act to move the forearm. They are made up of long strands of muscle tissue. Each strand is made up of thousands of muscle cells. When a muscle contracts, each cell in the muscle contracts. This action

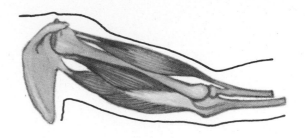

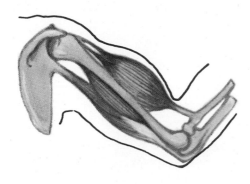

moves the bone or bones to which the muscle is attached. In order for the muscle cells to contract, they must have energy. Where does this energy come from?

Energy can be stored in the tissues which make up your muscles. Using your muscles a lot uses up stored energy very quickly. Can you explain why many sport activities have rest periods for the players?

As you look back at the activity you just did, do you know why the muscles which move the forearm contract at the same time? Do you know how the muscles in your digestive tube are able to move the food along? In order for your body to perform all the different actions it does, there must be some way of controlling the actions of the muscles. The system that controls all the activities of the body is the nervous (NUR-vuhs) system.

143

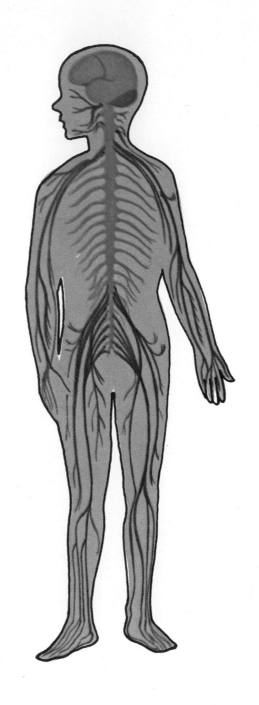

144

The nervous system is made up of organs called the brain, the spinal cord, the nerves, and the sense organs. Some nerves go from the place where a thing is touched or felt to the spinal cord and brain. Other nerves carry "messages" from the brain and spinal cord to the muscles and cause them to move. By means of these nerves you perform such activities as walking, writing, swimming, scratching, and using knives, forks, and spoons for eating.

Some parts of the nervous system tell your muscles to act without your knowing about it. Let us look at one of these actions.

30/Observe

Have one of your classmates sit so that he faces the windows in the room. Have him hold a clean handkerchief over one of his eyes for a minute. Now tell him to quickly take away the handkerchief. As he does this, look very carefully at the dark round area in the

middle of his eye. What kind of change do you see? Does your classmate know that this is happening? What do you think causes this change in his eye? Before telling him what you think has happened, exchange places and have your classmate do the activity. Share your observations and your ideas with the rest of the class. ■

An action which happens so quickly that you do not know about it until after it has taken place is called a reflex (REE-fleks) action. Can you name other reflex actions in the body. Why do you think we have reflex actions?

TESTING YOUR IDEAS

Slowly move your arm in all the directions you can. Which of the following statements do you think can be related to what you have just done?

Food gives the body the energy it needs.

Waste materials made when food is used by the cells are eventually removed by the body.

The system of the heart and blood tubes carries food to cells and removes wastes.

The skeletal system gives support to the system of muscles.

The system of muscles enables the skeleton to move.

The nervous system causes muscles to move.

WHAT IS HEALTHY GROWING?

Food is used in the body to give you energy to run, jump, sing, read, and grow. As you think back to how small you were a few years ago, you know that you have grown. You grow because food materials are used to make new cells in your body.

Do you keep track of how much you grow from month to month? If not, why not start now?

31/Measure

Tack a tapemeasure to the wall. Stand up straight with your back against the tapemeasure. Ask a class-mate to place a ruler on your head, as shown in the pictures, and measure your height in inches. Be sure the ruler is held level.

Cut a strip of colored paper 1/2 inch wide, and as tall as you are. All the girls in the class can tape their paper strips to one wall of the classroom. All the boys can tape their strips to another wall. How does the height of the boys and the height of the girls in the class compare? Are there more tall boys or more tall girls in the class? ■

By studying the pictures you have made, you can easily see that your classmates grow at different rates. Perhaps you are shorter than your friends this year, but someday you may be taller than they.

How old are you? How tall are you? How much do you weigh? Look at the chart on page 149. It tells you the average weights of some boys and girls according to their ages and heights. Do you weigh more or less than the average for your age and weight? How much do you think you have grown this past year?

You are still growing. Your body is making new cells and your bones are still being formed. The way you stand, sit, and walk will affect the way your bones form. Look at the drawings on this page. Explain how the children in the picture are helping or hurting good growth of their bodies. How can you improve your own growth?

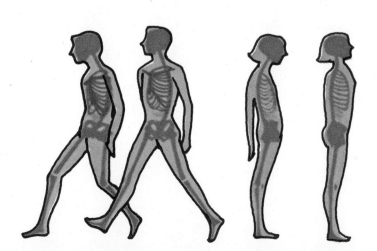

Average Weights

HEIGHT	9 YEARS	10 YEARS	11 YEARS
48″	53 lbs.	53 lbs.	
49″	55	55	55 lbs.
50″	58	58	58
51″	61	61	61
52″	64	64	64
53″	67	67	67
54″	70	70	70
55″	72	72	72
56″	76	76	76
57″	79	80	81
58″	83	84	84
59″		87	88
60″		91	92

GIRLS

HEIGHT	9 YEARS	10 YEARS	11 YEARS
48″	52 lbs.	53 lbs.	53 lbs.
49″	55	56	56
50″	58	59	61
51″	61	61	63
52″	64	64	65
53″	67	68	68
54″	70	70	71
55″	74	74	74
56″	76	78	78
57″	80	82	82
58″		84	86
59″		87	90
60″		91	95

Because you are yourself, you will be growing in your own special way. Because you are you, there is much you can do to make sure you stay healthy and grow properly. Do you sit, stand, and walk properly? Do you eat a balanced diet so that your body has the proper foods? Do you take care of your body? These are some of the things you can do to help yourself grow up to be healthy.

Your body is composed of cells which form tissues. The tissues go together as organs, and the organs form systems. The systems form a single living unit, an organism which is you. Throughout this unit you have been reminded that you are one single organism which is not like bricks laid together to make a wall. Your systems interact with each other in special ways, and some perform more than one function. You are not only a unit as an individual, you are unlike anyone else. You are the same single person from birth to death. The foods you eat now, the exercise you take, your posture, your habits of chewing, breathing, and training yourself in all the actions you can control will have an influence on you at present, and the influence of your present habits can extend throughout your future life.

A PROJECT FOR YOU

Proper health habits should be learned at an early age to insure a strong body and mind in adulthood. How do you care for yourself now? Make a list of the habits you have that make you strong. Also, make a list of any habits which you feel you should change. Finally, list habits you would like as an adult to keep your body healthy.

REVIEW

Below are listed particular statements about food and your growing body and general statements about them too. Which of the particular statements about food and your growing body are contained in each of the general statements? A general statement may explain more than one particular statement.

Particular Statement

1. Proteins are the main foods used to build and repair body tissue.
2. Without the muscular system, foods could not be digested.
3. A balanced diet is made up of four basic food groups, minerals, vitamins, and water.
4. Carbohydrates and fats are the main energy foods.
5. Without the system of capillaries, blood could not circulate.

General Statement

A. Your body must have the right kinds of food in order to grow properly.
B. Certain kinds of materials used by the body are found in foods.
C. The human body is made of systems working together as a unit.
D. A system is made of many parts working together as a unit.

Paula and Vera were testing a food to see if it contained starch, fat, or protein. Paula had grated the food into small pieces. Vera put some iodine into a bowl of water. The grated food was then mixed with the water. The color of the mixture turned blue-black.

"There!" said Vera. "The food contains starch!"

"Yes," said Paula, "that's true. But it might also contain fat or protein."

"Nonsense," Vera replied. "Iodine is a test for starch. There are no other things in the food."

"Isn't it possible?" Paula asked. "Why not do some tests?"

"We need no other tests," Vera commanded.

Was Vera wise not to test the food further? Try to explain your answer.

HOME PROJECTS

Construct models of the kinds of joints found in the body, using wood, screw hooks, and eyes. Show how the muscles move the bones in a hinge joint and in a ball-and-socket joint.

Obtain four hamsters and prepare a cage for each. Select healthy animals of the same size and age. To the first hamster feed a balanced diet made up of small amounts of vegetables, fruits, cereals, meat, and fat, such as butter. Feed the same diet to the second hamster, but do not include cereal foods. To the third hamster, feed the same diet but do not include meat, and to the fourth hamster, give everything on the diet except fruit and vegetables. Clean the cages daily and see that the animals have enough water. Run the experiment for three weeks, feeding the animals every four hours during the day, if possible. Keep a record of the weight and condition of each animal, and make a chart showing some of the changes you have observed.

LIBRARY RESEARCH

Examine a detailed illustration of the human body, showing organs, muscles, and bones. Find each of the major organs of the body, such as the lungs and heart, and then find some of the main systems. Be able to explain how each system helps the body. Look at drawings of the skeleton and the body's system of muscles, and determine in your mind how the muscles and bones work together. Be able to talk about the pictures that you have looked at and what each one represents.

Look up a good drawing of the circulatory system. Using tracing paper, draw it, using one color for the arteries and another for the veins. Display a drawing of the digestive system, which you have made in a similar manner, to your classmates. By means of arrows, show the movement of food through the digestive system. Be able to show both your charts and explain what is in them.

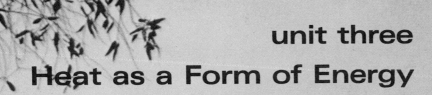

unit three
Heat as a Form of Energy

The sun shines down and warms the earth. Heat from the sun makes the earth suitable for living things, for plants and animals. At the beginning of man's history, his only source of heat was the sun. Men had to live in parts of the earth where the weather was always warm.

As time went on, people discovered other ways of keeping warm. They learned to make clothing from animal skins and plant fibers. They "tamed" the fires that started when lightning struck trees. They took some fire home with them to give heat during the cool night hours. They discovered that heat changes food, making it easier to chew. They learned to bake a clay pot in the fire to make it hard and waterproof.

Once men knew how to control heat, they did not have to depend on the sun for all their warmth. They could live in places where the weather was sometimes cold. They were free to travel and to settle in the cold lands. They were able to spread all over the earth.

How are you using heat right now? What kind of clothes are keeping you warm? What kind of food did you eat to keep your body warm? How was heat used to prepare the food? How is your classroom kept warm? Was heat used to make the furniture in the classroom? Do you suppose heat was used to make this book? Is heat still important in our modern-day world?

CAN HEAT CAUSE CHANGES?

Last year, you learned something about how chemists work. You learned about materials representing the three states of matter: solids, liquids, and gases. Most materials in our everyday world can be grouped as solids, liquids, and gases. Name some of each. Can a material be sometimes a solid and sometimes a liquid? What can make it change?

1/Observe

Put an ice cube in a pan and heat the pan on a hot plate. What is the state of matter of the ice cube? What happens to the ice cube when you heat it? Does

it change to a different state of matter? What do you call this state? Keep heating the pan. How many changes of state take place, in all? ■

Ice is water in the solid state. When ice is heated, it melts and becomes water. When water is heated, it boils and becomes a gas called water vapor. Water is one substance that is very familiar to us in all three states of matter. Have you ever changed liquid water to a solid? Can you change water vapor to a liquid?

2/Compare

Heat some water in a kettle until it boils. Put some ice into a small pan to cool the pan. Hold the side of the cool pan near the spout of the kettle. What do you see on the side of the pan?

What state was the water in as it came out of the kettle? What state was the water in after it touched the cold pan? ■

When a material gains enough heat, it may change from one state of matter to another. When a material loses enough heat, it may change from one state of matter to another. Which of the changes you observed were caused by gaining heat? Which were caused by losing heat?

Can heat change materials in another way? What would happen, for example, if you heated a solid but did not heat it enough to change its state?

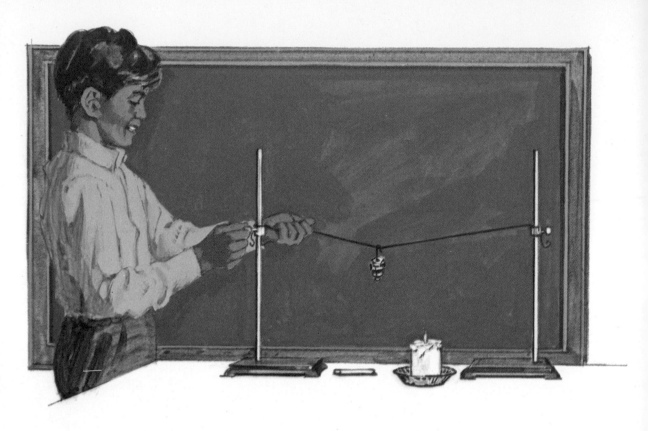

3/Observe

Take 3 feet of bare copper wire. Twist one end of the wire around the clamp of a ring stand. Hang a weight (a fishing sinker or a bunch of metal nuts) on the wire. Fasten the other end of the wire to another ring stand. Set this equipment on a table next to the chalkboard. Make a chalk mark where the weight hangs.

Your teacher will heat the wire. Where does the weight hang now? Make another mark on the chalkboard. What has happened to the length of the wire? Let the wire cool. What happens to its length now? ■

What will happen if you heat a liquid, but do not heat it enough to change its state?

4/Compare

Fill a small soda pop bottle with colored water. Use modeling clay to fasten a clear plastic straw into the top of the bottle, as the picture shows. Set the bottle in a small pan of water. Heat the pan and bottle on a hot plate. What do you see in the plastic straw?

With oven mitts on your hands, take the bottle out of the pan and put it on an asbestos pad. Let the bottle cool. What happens now in the plastic straw? ■

The wire is a solid. The colored water is a liquid. What was the same about the way heating changed them? Do you think that a gas will show the same kind of change when it is heated?

5/Observe

Put 2 or 3 drops of water into a large empty soda pop bottle. Fit a small balloon over the neck of the bottle as the picture shows. Heat the bottle in a pan of water on a hot plate. What happens to the balloon? Pick up the bottle with oven mitts and hold it in a bowl of cold water. What happens to the balloon now? ■

The length of the wire changed when it was heated. The water level in the plastic straw changed when the water in the bottle was heated. The size of the balloon changed when the air in the bottle was heated. What did you observe? How did all these things change?

In the language of science, we say that heating causes these materials to expand (eck-SPAND). From your observations, what do you think "expand" means?

When the wire lost heat, its length changed. When the water in the bottle lost heat, the water level in the straw changed. When the air in the bottle lost heat, the size of the balloon changed. What did you observe? How did all these things change?

In the language of science, we say that loss of heat causes these materials to contract (kun-TRAKT). From your observations, what do you think "contract" means?

When train tracks are put down, the rails are not placed tight against each other. A little space is left between one rail and the next. Then when the hot summer weather comes, there is room for the rails to expand. The pavement on highways has grooves in it for the same reason. If the grooves are not wide enough, or if the weather gets too hot, the paving may bump up, or "buckle." A metal bridge must be built so that one end is free to move. Then the metal of the bridge can expand in summer and contract in winter without damaging the bridge.

You have seen materials change from one state of matter to another as they gained and lost heat. You have seen materials expand and contract as they gained and lost heat. The materials changed in appearance, but they were still the same materials. Ice is water in the solid state, but it is still water. The copper wire gets longer and shorter as it is heated and cooled, but it is still copper wire.

When a material changes in appearance but is still the same material, the change is called a physical (FIZZ-i-k'l) change. From what you observed, can you say that heat causes physical changes?

TESTING YOUR IDEAS

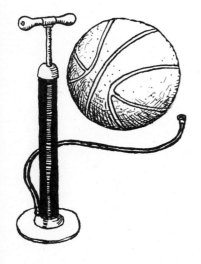

If a basketball is pumped up in a warm room and then taken outdoors on a cold day, will it get harder or softer? When you answer this question, use one of these words in your explanation: expand, contract.

WHAT OTHER CHANGES CAN HEAT CAUSE?

In activity 2, you heated water until it turned to water vapor. Then, with a cold pan, you turned the water vapor back to liquid water. Heat makes many kinds of changes. Can the changed material always be changed back again to its original form?

6/Compare

Put a spoonful of sugar in a metal jar lid. Heat the lid on a hot plate until the sugar melts and then chars. What color is the substance that is left? Does it look like sugar? Does it taste like sugar? When it cools, does it turn back to sugar? ■

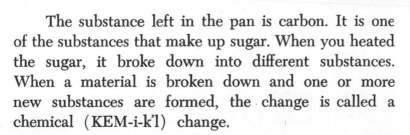

The substance left in the pan is carbon. It is one of the substances that make up sugar. When you heated the sugar, it broke down into different substances. When a material is broken down and one or more new substances are formed, the change is called a chemical (KEM-i-k'l) change.

7/Explain

Wash some steel wool in detergent and water. Rinse it thoroughly. Place the damp steel wool on a jar lid and leave it overnight. Look at it the next day. Touch it. Does it look the same? Does it feel the same? What do you see on your fingers? Has a new substance been formed? What kind of change has taken place? ■

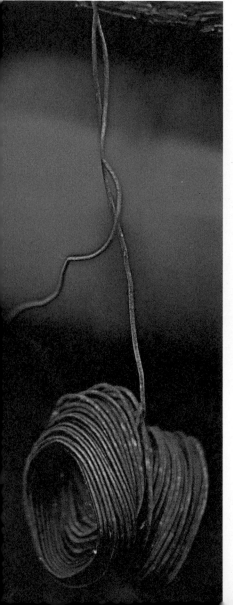

Steel is a form of iron. The iron combines with oxygen (AHK-si-j'n) in the air to form a new substance called rust. Another name for rust is iron oxide (AHK-side). Rusting is a slow combination of iron with oxygen. It produces a little heat, but so little that you cannot feel it. Fast combination with oxygen produces enough heat to feel—in fact, enough to burn!

Set a candle upright with modeling clay in an aluminum foil dish. Your teacher will light the candle and place an empty pint jar over it.

8/Observe

Touch the side of the jar very carefully and quickly. Is the candle producing heat? ■

When something burns, it joins quickly with oxygen. Did you notice the heat from this fast burning in

oxygen? If burning is a chemical change, one or more new substances must come from it. You can find out what they are.

9/Identify

Is the candle still burning inside the jar? Look at the inside surface of the jar. Do you see small drops of moisture? Can you guess what this moisture is?

Your teacher will pick up the jar with oven mitts and place it on a pad or pot holder. Cover the jar with a saucer and set it aside for a few minutes. When the jar has cooled, touch the moisture with your finger. Taste it. Now do you know what it is? ■

10/Identify

Your teacher will replace the jar over the burning candle. Leave it until the candle goes out. Using oven mitts, turn the dish and jar upside down. Take the dish away and quickly cover the jar with a lid. Lift the lid just far enough to let you pour some limewater into the jar. Then screw the lid on firmly and swirl the limewater around in the jar. What happens to the limewater? What gas do you think is in the jar? ■

These two activities tell you what new substances are formed when a candle burns. Is burning a chemical change? How do you know?

In activity 10, how long did it take for the candle to stop burning? Why did the candle stop burning?

Set up two candles in aluminum dishes. Your teacher will light them both, and then cover one with a pint jar and the other with a quart jar.

Record the time it takes for each to stop burning.

What do your records tell you? Which candle burned longer? What was different when the two candles started burning? What did one jar contain more of? ■

If burning is combining with oxygen, what will happen when most of the oxygen is used up? Can a material combine with oxygen when there is too little oxygen left?

For burning, three things are needed. First you must have a material that is able to burn. Was the candle wax able to burn? Why did it stop burning? The second thing you need is a supply of oxygen. Did the candles have a supply of oxygen? What happens when the supply is used up?

The third thing you need is heat. How did you start the candle burning? You can light a candle with a match, but can you set a log burning with just one match? Different materials start to burn at different temperatures. So you need not just *some* heat, but *enough* heat to start a particular material burning.

When you build a fire, you start with crumpled paper. Then you add some chips and small sticks of

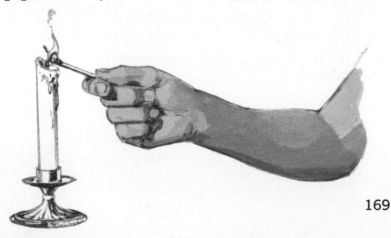

wood. On top of that, you put large sticks and small logs. A match sets fire to the paper. The burning paper produces enough heat to start the chips and small sticks burning. The burning sticks and chips give off enough heat to start the big sticks and small logs burning. When the small logs are burning, the fire is hot enough for a big log.

Jack blew some air into a balloon. He put the balloon on a sunny windowsill. The balloon got bigger.

Rose left her bicycle out in the rain. It got rusty.

Peter and Emily built a snowman in their backyard. After a week, it had melted away.

When Tom's Boy Scout troop went camping, they burned some wood to cook their dinner.

Which of these changes were caused by gaining or losing heat? Which were physical changes? Which were chemical changes?

HOW DOES HEAT TRAVEL THROUGH SOLIDS?

When you boil water in a pan, how does the heat get through the pan to the water? How does heat get to you from the heating unit on the other side of the classroom? How does heat get from the sun to the earth? How does heat travel? You can find out about the way heat travels by doing a few activities.

12/Observe

At lunchtime today, put a metal spoon into a bowl of hot soup. Leave it there for a few minutes. From time to time, touch the handle of the spoon. What do you notice? Does heat travel through the spoon? ■

The metal spoon carries the heat of the soup to your hand. Which was hotter, the soup or the spoon? Which was hotter, the spoon or your hand? Which way does the heat travel: from hot to cold or from cold to hot?

13/Observe

Pour some very hot water into a metal cup. Touch the cup with your hand. What do you feel? Which is hotter, the cup or your hand? In which direction is heat traveling?

Pour some very cold water into a metal cup. Touch the cup with your hand. What do you feel? Which is hotter, the cup or your hand? In which direction is heat traveling? ■

Do you think it is true to say that heat travels from a place where there is more heat to a place where there is less heat? The spoon and the cup were both made of metal. Both of them were made of solid materials. How does heat travel through solid materials?

172

14/Test

Take a solid metal curtain rod. Attach tacks to it with a few drops of candle wax. Space the tacks about 2 inches apart. Watch as your teacher holds one end of the rod in a flame. Which tack drops off first? In what order do the rest of the tacks fall off? Which one falls off last? What does this test tell you about the way heat travels through the rod? ■

15/Model

Take six of these textbooks. Set them up on a table top about 4 inches apart. Look at the picture. Tap the first book just hard enough to knock it over. What happens to the rest of the books? How is this model like what happened in activity 14? Does heat seem to be passed on from one portion of the rod to the next? ■

This method is the way heat travels in solid materials. It is called conduction (kun-DUCK-shun). Do all solid materials conduct heat at the same speed?

16/Compare

Cut off a 7-inch piece of the curtain rod you used in activity 14. Get three other rods of the same size, but of different materials. Another metal, wood, and glass are good examples.

Make four holes in the lid of a coffee can. The holes should be just big enough to hold the rods. Pour 1 inch of water into the can and put the lid on the can. Push one rod through each hole so that the end of the rod is in the water. Use wax to attach a tack to the upper end of each rod.

Put the can on a hot plate. Heat the water in the can. Which tack drops off first? Which one drops off last? Which material is the best conductor of heat? Which is the poorest conductor of heat? ■

Different solids conduct heat at different speeds. Metals are generally good conductors of heat. Heat travels through them fast. Wood is a poor conductor. Heat travels through it much more slowly. Materials that are poor conductors of heat are called insulators (IN-suh-late'rz).

Are the walls of your home insulated? How do you suppose insulated walls help to keep your home warmer in winter and cooler in summer? Why do metal cooking pots often have wooden handles? What is the use of pot holders?

17/Compare

Fill the metal cup with very cold water again. Fill a plastic cup of the same size with very cold water. Touch the metal cup with your left hand. Touch the plastic cup with your right hand. Which hand feels colder? Which cup is conducting heat away from your

hand faster? Which is the better conductor? Which is the better insulator? Which material would make a better pot? Which would make a better handle for a pot? ■

Suppose you made a campfire to toast marshmallows. You looked around for something you could use to hold the marshmallows in the fire. You found a long thin metal rod and a long thin wooden stick. Which would you use for toasting the marshmallows? Explain your choice.

TESTING YOUR IDEAS

The picture below shows two metal rods. Rod A is one single piece of metal. Rod B has had a section cut out of it and replaced with wood. Both rods have tacks attached to them with candle wax at the right-hand end. Both rods are being heated at the left-hand end. Which tack will fall off first, the one on rod A or the one on rod B? When you explain your prediction, use the words conduct and insulate.

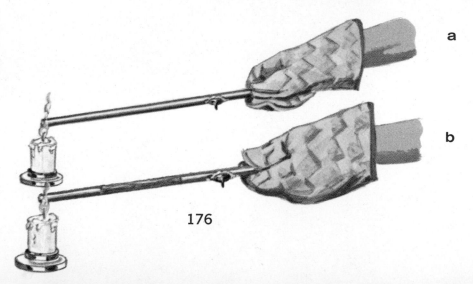

a

b

HOW DOES HEAT TRAVEL THROUGH LIQUIDS AND GASES?

You have tested some solid materials to find out how they conduct heat. Now test a common liquid, water.

18/Test

Drop a small piece of ice into a test tube and wedge it in place with some steel wool. Fill the test tube with water. The steel wool will hold the ice in place but will let the water pass through.

Watch while your teacher heats the test tube over a flame. Notice that the test tube is being heated at the top, as the picture shows. When the water at the top

of the test tube is boiling, look at the bottom of the tube. If the ice has not melted away, what can you say about water as a conductor of heat? ■

If you had time to make enough tests, you would find that almost all liquids, except liquid metals like mercury, are poor heat conductors. How about gases? Air is the most common gas. Is air a good heat conductor?

19/Compare

Your teacher will light a candle. Hold your hand about 10 inches above the candle flame. Can you feel the heat? Now hold your hand 10 inches from the side of the flame. Do you feel the heat? Is heat traveling sideways from the candle flame? ■

Air is all around the flame. If air conducts heat, you should find no difference at the same distance above and to the sides of the flame. Is air a good or poor conductor of heat? There is a layer of air between the storm window and the regular window of a house. How does this air space help to insulate the house?

You have tested the heat properties of a common liquid and a common gas. What have you discovered about them as conductors of heat? Liquids and gases can be grouped under the name of fluids (FLOO-idz). You see every day that heat can travel through water and through air. If it does not travel by conduction, how does heat travel through fluids?

178

20/Observe

Wrap a few turns of wire around a candle. Leave
about 15 inches of wire for a handle. Bend the handle
straight up next to the candle and bend the end of it
into a hook. Your teacher will light the candle and
lower it into a milk bottle by its wire handle. What
happens to the candle flame in a little while?

Take the candle out of the bottle. Blow into the
bottle two or three times to change the air in the bottle.
Cut a T-shaped piece out of cardboard. The stem of
the T should just fit into the neck of the milk bottle.
Your teacher will light the candle and lower it into the
bottle again. Quickly put the cardboard T into the
neck of the bottle. What happens to the candle flame
this time?

Is there a difference? Why? Your teacher will light
one end of a piece of rope and then blow out the flame.

While the rope is still smoking, hold it next to one side of the T. Where does the smoke go? Now hold the smoking rope on the other side of the T. Where does the smoke go? ■

Hot air is carrying the smoke upward on one side of the T. What is happening on the other side? The smoke shows that cool air is sinking into the bottle on the other side of the T. The upward and downward drafts of air are called convection (kun-VECK-shun) currents. Heat travels through fluids by the method called convection.

To understand the reason for convection currents in fluids, you must understand the meaning of the word "dense." What do you think of when you read about a "dense forest"? The word "dense" can be applied to all matter. Let's find out why.

21/Compare

Weigh a brick and record the weight. Measure the brick carefully and cut a large sponge to the exact same size as the brick. Weigh the sponge and record its weight. Which weighs more, the brick or the sponge? Which weighs less? ■

The brick and the sponge occupy exactly the same amount of space. Which one weighs more? When you have two things that are exactly the same size, but differ in weight, then they have different densities (DEN-si-teez). The one with the greater weight for the same size has the greater density. The one with the lower weight for the same size has the lower density.

Now apply this idea to fluids. You know that water and air expand when they are heated and therefore become less dense. If you poured a cupful of very hot water and let it cool, you would have a little less than a cupful of cool water. If you measured out a cupful of very hot water and a cupful of cold water, the cupful of very hot water would weigh a little less.

The cupful of cold water, being a little bit heavier than the cupful of hot water would really have a little more water in it. Cold water is denser than hot water. Likewise, cold air is denser than hot air. The greater weight of the denser material makes it fall to the bottom of the container. It pushes up the less dense material. Can you use these facts to explain what you saw happening in activity 20?

Convection takes place in fluids because different parts of the fluid have different densities. The different densities result from one part of the fluid being heated more than another. What happens when you heat a pot of water unevenly?

22/Observe

Fill a Pyrex glass coffee pot with water. Set the pot on a hot plate so that only one side of the pot is on the heating unit. Look at the picture. When the water has come to a full boil, add a teaspoonful of sawdust to the water in the pot. The sawdust will help you to see the movement of the water. Where is there a down current? Where is the water being heated? Where is there an up current? Is heat traveling through the water or are different parts of the water actually moving? ■

181

Cut some narrow streamers of very thin tissue paper. Tape them to the end of a long stick. Use this stick to test for air currents in different parts of the classroom. But first, tell what you expect to find in each place you will test.

23/Predict

What do you expect to find near the top of an open window? What do you expect to find near the bottom of an open window? What do you expect to find near the heating unit or air conditioner? Test these places and as many others as you can think of. Were your guesses correct? ■

If you have a window that opens at top and bottom, how would you arrange the openings to get the best circulation of air?

182

In activity 18, water was boiled in a test tube containing an ice cube. Explain what happened, in terms of convection currents.

In activity 19, you held your hand 10 inches above a candle flame, and then 10 inches to the side of the candle flame. Explain what you observed, in terms of convection.

HOW DOES HEAT TRAVEL THROUGH SPACE?

The sun is far off in space. There is no solid material between the earth and the sun. There is no liquid or gas filling the space between the earth and the sun. How does heat travel from the sun to the earth? Heat travels in solids by conduction. Heat travels through fluids by convection. But how does heat travel through airless space?

24/Observe

Move your hand around an unlighted electric bulb. Do you feel any heat from it in any position? Turn the light on and move your hand around the bulb again. In which position do you feel the heat from the bulb?

What is between the bulb and your hand? Where must your hand be to receive heat from the bulb by convection? Did you feel heat from the bulb when your hand was in any other position? ■

Heat travels in all directions from any hot object. This kind of heat travel is called radiation (ray-dee-AY-shun). When heat travels by radiation, it moves outward from the hot object without needing a solid or a fluid to carry it.

Hold your hand in the sunlight. Do you feel warmth? Does heat come from the sun? What happens to the heat that radiates from hot objects? What happens to heat from the sun? What happens when it strikes an object on the earth?

25/Compare

a. Place two thermometers in the sunlight. Put a white cloth over one thermometer and a black cloth over the other. Every 5 minutes for half an hour, read and record the temperature on each thermometer.

b. Fill two pint jars with cool water. Wrap white paper around one jar. Wrap black paper around the other jar. Put a thermometer in each jar. Place both jars in the sunlight. Read and record the temperature in each jar every 15 minutes for one hour.

c. Collect a lot of cans, all exactly the same size. Make cardboard covers for them. Each cover should have a hole just big enough to let a thermometer fit snugly through. Paint one can black, using "flat" paint. Paint one can white. Leave one can shiny. Paint the other cans as many different colors as you have paint for. Fill the cans with water. Put a cardboard cover on each can. Put a thermometer in each can. Wait 5 minutes and then record the temperature for each can. Put the cans in the sunlight. Wait 15 minutes and then record the temperature for each can again. Which can showed the greatest difference between the first and second temperature? Which showed the least? ■

186

When radiated heat strikes an object, what happens depends on the kind of surface the object has. Heat bounces off some surfaces; we say it is reflected (ree-FLECK-ted). Heat sinks into some surfaces; we say it is absorbed (ab-SORBD). In the activities you just did, what kind of surface seemed to reflect heat? What kind of surface seemed to absorb heat? From what you have seen, do you think you can guess what will happen in the next activity?

26/Predict

With a can opener, remove the top and bottom from a large juice can. Paint one half of the can black, inside and out. Leave the other half of the can shiny. With candle wax, fasten a tack to the black side of the can. Fasten another tack to the shiny side of the can. Your teacher will place the can over a lighted candle. Which tack would you think will fall off first? Watch and see whether your guess was correct. ■

Was your prediction right? Which side of the can absorbed more heat? Which side reflected more heat?

Have you ever taken a Thermos bottle on a picnic? How does a Thermos bottle keep the milk cold until you are ready to drink it? Look at the picture which shows the layers of a Thermos bottle.

The outside layer is made of metal or plastic. The center section is made of glass. Both the glass and the inside of the metal or plastic case have a shiny coating, like a mirror. Most of the air has been pumped out of the space between the outer case and the center section.

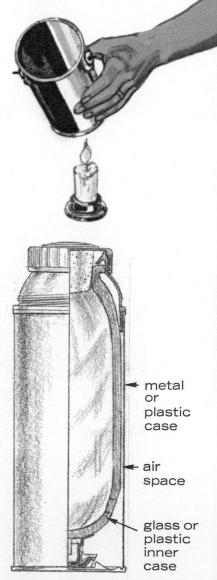

metal or plastic case

air space

glass or plastic inner case

187

Metal and plastic are both solids. How does heat travel through solids? Would a space that is almost empty of air conduct heat? Would heat travel by convection through such a space? What type of heat travel does not need a solid or a fluid? What does a shiny surface do to radiated heat?

Now can you explain: How does a Thermos bottle keep drinks cold? How does it stop all three methods of heat travel? If you filled a Thermos bottle with hot soup, would it keep the soup hot? Why?

At the beach on a hot day, which will give you more protection from the sun's heat: a white jacket or a black jacket?

Why do astronauts wear white suits? How does heat travel to a spacecraft from the sun?

HOW DO WE MEASURE TEMPERATURE?

What is hot? Can you tell? Can you *always* tell? Try this and see.

27/Compare

Take three large bowls. Fill the first with cold water and add a few ice cubes to make the water very cold. Fill the second bowl with lukewarm water. Fill the third with hot water, not too hot for your hand to touch.

Put your left hand in the bowl of cold water. Put your right hand in the bowl of hot water. Leave them there for two minutes. Then put both hands at once into the bowl of lukewarm water.

How does the lukewarm water feel to your left hand? How does it feel to your right hand? Is there a difference? ■

Is your temperature sense exact? Does your temperature sense tell you "exactly 72 degrees"? Or does it say "hotter than this, less hot than that"? Why are hot and cold not exact terms? To know exactly how hot or cold something is, you use a thermometer. How can a thermometer show the exact temperature?

Most of the thermometers you use contain a liquid.

28/Mark

Fill an empty soda pop bottle with colored water. Hold a plastic straw in the neck of a bottle with modeling clay. Press down on the clay so that the colored water rises in the tube about 3 inches above the stopper.

Place the bottle in a pan of water and heat it on a hot plate. Allow the water in the pan to boil. When the colored water has stopped rising in the straw, mark the water level with a felt-tipped pen.

Take the bottle out of the pan, using oven mitts. Do not shake the bottle. Let it cool to room temperature. Then put it into a deep bowl. Fill the bowl with ice. Pack the ice around the bottle. Watch the water in the straw. Which way does it move? When it has stopped moving, mark the water level.

The two marks give you a high point and a low point for a temperature scale. This method is like the way a thermometer is marked.

When you mark a thermometer, you first find the level to which the liquid expands when it is heated to the temperature of boiling water. Then you find the level to which the liquid contracts when it is cooled to the temperature of melting ice. These two levels are called the fixed points of the thermometer. You can make a scale from these points when you have learned more about thermometers.

The thermometer scale we use in everyday life in the United States is the Fahrenheit (FAR-en-hite) thermometer scale. It was invented in the beginning of the 18th century by Gabriel Fahrenheit, a German physicist. For the low point of his scale, he took the temperature of a mixture of ice and salt, and marked it zero degrees. The sign for degrees is °. Temperatures on the Fahrenheit scale are followed by the letter F. We can write zero degrees Fahrenheit as 0°F.

For a high point, Fahrenheit used what he thought was the normal temperature of the human body, and marked it 96°F. He made a scale from his fixed points. Using his scale, he found the temperature of boiling water to be 212°F, and the temperature of melting ice to be 32°F.

At about the same time, Anders Celsius (SELL-see-us), a Swedish astronomer, invented another thermometer scale. Temperatures on this scale are followed by the letter C. He marked the freezing and boiling points of water 0°C and 100°C. Scientists all over the world use the Celsius scale.

The Celsius scale is also called the centigrade (SENT-uh-grade) scale. "Centigrade" means "one

Celsius

191

hundred steps." Do you think this is a good name for a scale that has one hundred degrees between its fixed points? How many degrees are there between the fixed points of the Fahrenheit scale?

Look at the diagram of the two scales. How many degrees does each line on each scale represent? What Celsius temperature is equal to 68°F? These are comfortable indoor temperatures. What Celsius temperature is equal to 0°F?

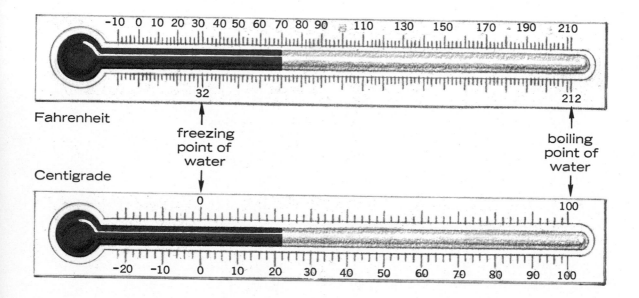

Fahrenheit

freezing
point of
water

boiling
point of
water

Centigrade

You should be able now to make either a Fahrenheit or Celsius thermometer scale by using the fixed points that you marked on the straw in activity 28. What liquid did you use in your thermometer? Why did you color it? Most liquid thermometers use alcohol or mercury. Why is water not a useful liquid for thermometers?

The table shows the freezing and boiling temperatures of two common thermometer liquids. Which liquid would be more useful if you wanted to measure temperatures at the North Pole? Could you use an alcohol thermometer to measure the temperature of boiling water?

	FREEZING POINT	BOILING POINT
Mercury	−40°F	675°F
Alcohol	−175°F	172°F

ARE THERE DIFFERENT THERMOMETERS?

The thermometer you made in activity 28 is a liquid thermometer. The thermometer shown in the margin is a liquid thermometer, too. It is marked with the Fahrenheit scale. What part of the full scale is shown? Look at the scale of the thermometer in the picture. Each degree is divided into five parts. Each line stands for two tenths of a degree. To read a temperature on this thermometer, you say the last whole number before the end of the liquid column. Then you count the number of tenths until you reach the end of the liquid column.

What temperature is shown on the thermometer in the picture? This is the average body temperature for man. What did Fahrenheit think was the normal temperature of the human body?

Some people may have a normal temperature a little above or a little below 98.6°F. Usually a tempera-

ture above 98.6°F means that you have a fever. Why is this thermometer sometimes called a fever thermometer? Why does a fever thermometer show only 92°F to 110°F?

In most liquid thermometers, the liquid can move freely up and down. If the mercury started to go down as soon as you took the thermometer out of your mouth, could you ever know exactly what your temperature was? Notice that the tube holding the liquid is pinched together near the bottom. The mercury cannot fall back past this pinched place. You have to shake the thermometer hard to force the mercury down.

Another kind of thermometer is a gas thermometer. You can make one with a soda pop bottle. Fix a clear plastic straw in the neck of a bottle with modeling clay. Be sure that the straw and clay are airtight. Wire or tap the bottle to the side of a large carton, as shown in the picture. Tape a strip of paper to the carton next to the plastic straw. You will mark your scale on this paper.

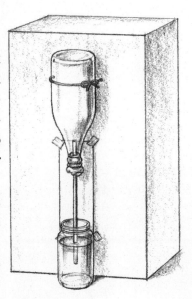

Put the free end of the straw into a jar of colored cold water. Heat the bottle gently with an unshaded lamp or with your hands to drive out some of the air. Let the bottle cool. When the bottle cools, the colored water should be about halfway up the straw.

29/Measure

To make a scale for your gas thermometer, let it stand for half an hour in a warm place. Put an ordinary indoor-outdoor thermometer beside it. Mark the level of the water on the paper. Next to the mark, write the temperature that the indoor-outdoor thermometer shows. Put the two thermometers in a cool place for half an hour. Mark the water level again and write the temperature next to this mark.

How many fixed points do you have on your scale? How many degrees difference is there between these fixed points? Divide the space between the marks on the paper into the proper number of degrees.

Rub your hands together until they become very warm. Gently place them around the bottle. When the water stops moving in the straw, where does it reach on the scale? Are your hands hotter or cooler than the highest temperature on the scale? Can you read the temperature of your hands on the scale? ■

What material expands in a fever thermometer to show the temperature? What material expands in an indoor-outdoor thermometer to show the temperature? What material expands in this gas thermometer? Where are the higher numbers on the scale of the gas thermometer? Is the gas thermometer different in this way from a liquid thermometer?

You have shown that gases expand when they are heated. The gas thermometer uses this expansion to show temperature. The expanding gas in the bottle pushes on the liquid in the straw. The higher the temperature, the more the gas expands. Where are the higher numbers on the scale of the gas thermometer?

What temperatures does an oven thermometer show? Would air be a good expansion material in an oven thermometer? Would alcohol? Would mercury?

Most oven thermometers work by the expansion and contraction of a bar made of two kinds of metal. When the bar is heated, one metal expands more than the other. When the bar cools, one metal contracts more than the other. Make a model of a metal thermometer to see how it works.

196

Take some wrapping paper that is metal foil on one side and paper on the other. Cut a strip that is three inches long and 3/4 inch wide. Tape the strip to the top of a cardboard box. Cut a pointer from lightweight cardboard and staple it to the end of the foil-paper strip. Look at the drawing to see how the instrument should look when it is finished.

30/Test

Place the instrument on a warm radiator. What happens to the strip? In which direction does the pointer move? Mark that side of the box WARMER. Put the instrument in a refrigerator. In which direction does the pointer move? Mark that side of the box COOLER. What is happening to the foil-paper strip? ■

When the foil-paper strip is heated, the foil expands more than the paper. What happens to the strip? When the foil-paper strip is cooled, the foil contracts more than the paper. What happens to the strip?

TESTING YOUR IDEAS

Which gives you more readings on the Fahrenheit scale, a fever thermometer or an indoor-outdoor thermometer?

Where are the higher temperatures shown on the scale of a gas thermometer?

Where are the higher temperatures shown on the scale of the model metal thermometer that you made?

How are the gas and metal thermometers different from the liquid thermometer? How are they all alike?

WHAT IS HEAT?

Heat can be passed on from one part of an object to another part of the same object. It can travel from one object to another object. It flows from one place to another place. What is heat?

Aristotle (AR-uh-staht'l) was a Greek who lived in the 4th century B.C. He taught that everything in the world was made up of four basic materials: earth, air, fire, and water. Some objects had more fire and some had less. The more fire an object contained, the hotter it was.

Over the centuries, ideas changed. By the time that Gabriel Fahrenheit and Anders Celsius were making their thermometer scales, heat was thought to be a fluid. The fluid was called caloric (ka-LOR-ick) and it was thought to be present in every material. Some materials had more of it and some had less. Caloric flowed from warm objects to cooler ones. You could squeeze caloric out of materials. You could add caloric to materials by holding them over flames. Ice combined with caloric to form water.

Some thinkers did not agree with the caloric explanation of heat. One of them was Benjamin Thompson, Count Rumford, an American who was the minister of war of Bavaria in the late 18th century. He suspected that heat was not a form of material. Materials, he reasoned, had weight. If heat were particles or a fluid, it would have weight. A warm material would weigh more than a cold one.

Rumford

199

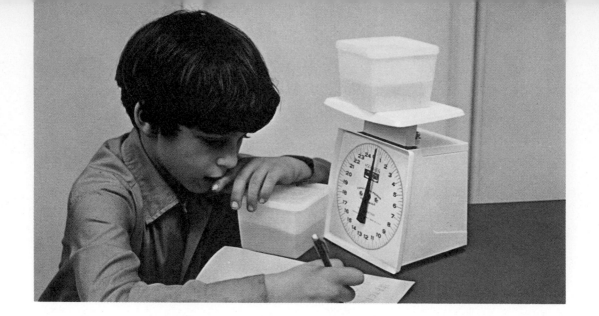

31/Compare

Measure one cup of water exactly. Pour it into a plastic freezer container. Cover the container tightly so that no water can get in or out. Put the container into a freezer until the water has frozen solid.

Measure another cup of water exactly. Pour it into a plastic freezer container that is exactly like the first one you used. Again, cover the container tightly. Leave the container on a table or shelf until the water has come to room temperature. It should take about one hour.

Weigh the container of water at room temperature. Record this weight. Take the other container out of the freezer. If any frost has formed on the outside of the container, wipe it off. What do you expect to find when you weigh this container? Weigh it, and record the weight. Compare the two weights that you recorded. Which container lost heat? Did it lose weight also? Does heat seem to have weight? ■

Rumford tried many experiments. He filled jars with alcohol and water, and placed them in rooms with temperatures hot enough to boil the liquids or cold enough to freeze them. He weighed the jars and compared their weights, but he could find no signs that heat had weight.

As part of his job as minister of war, Rumford had to inspect the places where cannons were made. He watched the workmen as they took a solid brass rod and drilled a hole down the length of the rod. During the drilling, the brass got very hot.

Count Rumford asked himself where this heat came from. He measured the temperature of chips of metal that were drilled out of the rod. They were hotter than boiling water! But the metal was not changed in any way. The only change that happened during the making of the cannon was the movement of the drill against the metal. Did the movement cause the heat? Is there a connection between heat and motion?

32/Test

Rub your hands together. What do you feel? Rub a pencil eraser on a sheet of paper while you count slowly to twenty. Then touch the eraser to your cheek. What do you feel? ■

Are you really heating things by rubbing them together, or do they just feel hot? Measure, and find out.

33/Measure

Hold an indoor-outdoor thermometer between your hands until the liquid column stops rising. Record the temperature it shows. Rub your hands together hard while you count slowly to two hundred. Again hold the thermometer between your hands until the liquid stops rising. Are your hands actually hotter after rubbing them together, or do they only feel that way? ■

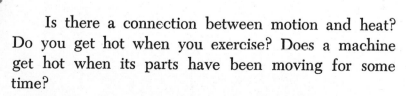

Is there a connection between motion and heat? Do you get hot when you exercise? Does a machine get hot when its parts have been moving for some time?

What do you think will happen in the following case? You have a pitcher full of water. You measure out exactly one cup of water into each of two bowls. The bowls are exactly the same. You put one ice cube into each bowl. You leave one bowl alone until the ice cube melts. You stir the water in the other bowl until the ice cube melts.

Do the ice cubes in both bowls melt in the same amount of time?

Does one melt before the other? If so, which one melts first?

Try it and find out if your prediction was right.

IS HEAT A FORM OF ENERGY?

When you studied machines and work, you learned that the word "work" has a special meaning in the language of science. Work is done when something is moved a certain distance. You can push on a brick wall until you are tired out, but you won't be doing any work—unless you *move* the wall! On the other hand, if you push a book across your desk, you are doing work.

You need energy to do work. Can heat do work? Can heat move things? Is heat energy?

When you warmed the air in the gas thermometer, what happened? Did something move a certain distance? When you put a fever thermometer in your mouth, what happens? Does something move a certain distance?

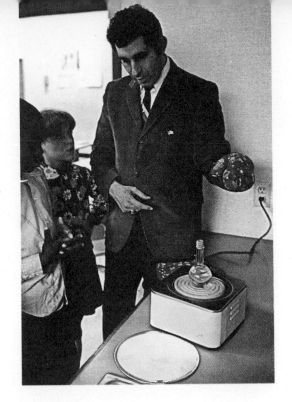

34/Observe

Pour one inch of water into a Pyrex glass flask. Put a cork into the neck of the flask and push it down lightly. Do not press hard on the cork. Watch while your teacher heats the flask on a hot plate. When the water has been boiling for a little while, what happens? Does something move a certain distance? ▪

Can heat do work? Do you think it is fair to say that heat is energy? What other kinds of energy do you know of? Do they all move things a large or small distance?

You saw that heat is connected with the energy of motion. Do you suppose there is a connection between heat and some other kinds of energy? Does heat cause chemical changes? Do you think there might be a connection between heat and chemical energy? What happens when you plug in an electric iron? Can electrical energy produce heat?

Herschel

Is there a connection between heat and light energy? In 1800, this question was asked by Sir William Herschel (HERR-shell), an English scientist. He was studying light so that he could learn more about the sun and the stars. He knew that when he held a prism in a beam of light, the white light was broken up into all the colors of the rainbow.

Herschel measured the temperature of each color of light coming out of a prism. He found that the red light had the highest temperature. Then he moved the thermometer below the red, where there was no light to be seen. Surprise! This was by far the hottest place!

You can do Sir William Herschel's experiment. Choose a window where the sun shines in. Cover it with black construction paper, except for a slit 1/2 inch wide and 2 inches long. Draw the shades on the other windows to darken the room as much as possible. Turn a prism in the beam of light until the light makes a rainbow on the wall. Then fasten the prism to a stand. Put a piece of white cardboard close to the prism so that the rainbow shows on the cardboard.

35/Measure

Take an indoor-outdoor thermometer that is at room temperature. Tape the thermometer to the cardboard so that the red light is shining on the thermometer bulb. Wait 5 minutes. You may have to move the cardboard to keep the red light exactly on the thermometer bulb. After 5 minutes, record the temperature that the thermometer shows.

Move the thermometer and tape it to the cardboard so that the bulb is just below the red band of light. Wait 5 minutes. Check the temperature. Is it higher or lower than when the bulb was in red light? ■

206

There seems to be some radiation that we cannot see, but that is real, all the same. We call it infrared (in-fruh-RED), which means "below red." Infrared rays are given off by all hot objects. Have you ever used a heater that gave off lots of heat, but very little light? Was it giving off infrared rays? Kitchens on airplanes cook dinners very quickly in infrared ovens.

We live in a world full of energy and of energy changes. When you turn on a lamp, electrical energy is changed to light energy and some heat energy. The chemical energy stored in the food you eat is changed to the energy of your muscles. When you use muscular energy, you give off some heat energy, too. When you strike a gong, the energy of motion is changed to sound energy. Hit the gong many times in a row, and it will become warm at the spot where you strike it. Whenever any kind of energy is used, some of it is changed to heat energy.

TESTING YOUR IDEAS

What do scientists mean by "work"?
Can heat do work?
Is heat energy?

HOW IS HEAT ENERGY
CONNECTED WITH MOTION?

How many states of matter do you know? In grade 3 you examined rocks. Some rocks were made of small bits stuck together. Some rocks seemed to be one solid piece, but you could break the rock into smaller and smaller pieces. Are these very small pieces still rock? Are there other materials made of pieces?

36/Observe

Fill a glass to the top with water. Look at it carefully. Do you see any spaces in the water? Do you see any pieces of water? Carefully pour a level teaspoonful of sugar into the water. What happens? How many teaspoonsful of sugar can you drop into the glass of water before it overflows? ■

Do you think there are spaces in water? Could water be made up of tiny pieces, too small to see? Let's test the idea.

37/Measure

Put a drop of black ink into a glass of water. How long does it take for the ink to spread throughout the water? ■

You did not stir the water. Yet the black ink seemed to move through the water. Do you think gases mix together in the same way as liquids do? Can you smell gas in the living room if there is gas leaking in the kitchen? How do you know when someone has used perfume? Do gases seem to mix?

Will solids spread through each other? Here is an experiment that has been done in science laboratories, with special equipment.

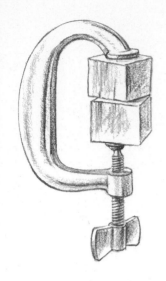

A block of gold and a block of lead were held together for a long time by a machine called a vise. After a long time, the surfaces that touched were examined. Gold was found in the surface of the lead block. Lead was found in the surface of the gold block. Some gold had moved into the lead and some lead had moved into the gold.

Is this example like the black ink moving through the water? Is it like the gas moving through the air? Something moved in each form of matter. Some matter spread through other matter without a push or pull from outside the matter.

Matter acts as if it is made up of tiny moving pieces, so different materials mix with each other. These pieces must be very small, for you cannot see them. Even when you look at water through a microscope, you cannot see pieces of water. Of course, you may see pieces *in* the water.

Think of how much sugar you poured into the glass full of water before it overflowed. The sugar took up space, so there must be space between these tiny moving pieces. Many times, scientists will say, "It seems as if." You can say, from what you have observed, "*It seems as if* matter is made up of tiny moving pieces with spaces between them."

38/Explain

Fill a drinking glass with marbles. Is the glass full? Are there spaces between the marbles? Sift a handful of sand into the glass. Where docs the sand go? Does this model help you to explain how materials mix with each other? ■

210

You have learned that there is a connection between heat and motion. If this is true, then there should be a connection between heat and matter, which acts as if it is made up of tiny moving particles.

39/Compare

Repeat activity 37. Put a drop of black ink into a glass of cold water. At the same time, put a drop of black ink into a glass of hot water. How long does it take for the ink to move through the cold water? How long does it take for the ink to move through the hot water? Which period of time is shorter? Can you guess why? ■

Can you conclude that matter is made of tiny pieces? Your activities show that tiny particles of matter are moving. Heat seems to increase their motion. You observed that the black ink moved through hot water faster than through cold water.

40/Predict

Take two cups. Put a teaspoonful of instant coffee in each cup. Fill one cup with cold water and the other with hot water. In which cup will the instant coffee mix faster? ■

Is cocoa easier to make with hot milk or cold milk? When do you think odors would spread faster, on a hot day or a cold day?

Count Rumford thought that heat was connected with motion, but he could not explain how. Can you?

Look back at activity 14/Test on page 173. What did you find out when you did the activity? Suppose the rod is made up of tiny moving pieces? Where would the pieces be moving fastest? Where would they be moving slowest? Can you use the idea of tiny moving pieces to explain what happened in activity 14?

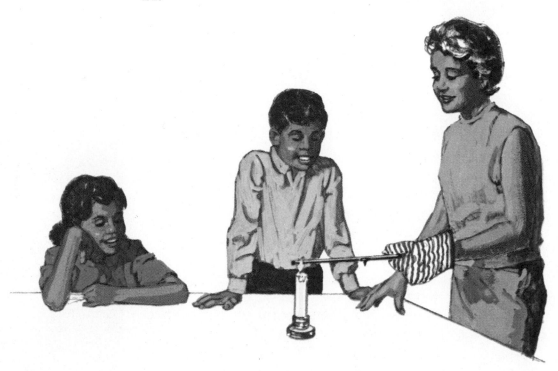

Water can be a solid, a liquid, or a gas. What makes the difference? What kind of change do you call this? What do you mean when you say that heating makes materials expand?

What kind of change is burning? Is a new substance formed when something burns? What three things are needed for burning? Do you think you could stop a fire by taking away one of these three things?

How does heat travel through solids? Does heat travel through all solid materials at the same speed? What is an insulator? How are insulators used?

Name some fluids. How does heat travel through fluids? Do fluids conduct heat? Look at the fluids at the side of the page. Which is denser, A or B?

How does heat travel through space? What kinds of surfaces absorb heat? What kinds of surfaces reflect heat?

How does a thermometer work? Does a thermometer depend on the fact that heat can travel? Does a thermometer depend on the fact that heat makes things expand? How do you make a scale for a thermometer?

213

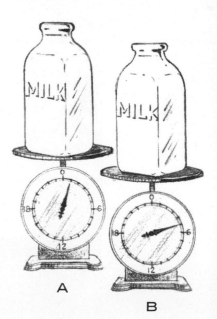

A

B

Draw a picture of a Thermos bottle. Show how it prevents heat from traveling in the three ways you learned about.

Is there a connection between heat and motion? Show how motion can produce heat. Tell how heat can produce motion.

What does a scientist mean when he talks about "work"? Can heat do work? Is there a connection between heat and some other kinds of energy? Is there a connection between heat and light?

HOME PROJECTS

How long can you keep an ice cube? What materials do you know of that do not conduct heat? How can you prevent heat from traveling by convection? by radiation? Design and make an ice-cube keeper. Have a contest with your friends to see whose design will keep an ice cube longest.

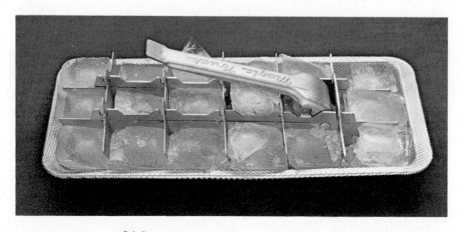

a. Wood's ability   is greater than   Iron's ability
   to conduct heat   is the same as   to conduct
                      is less than   heat

b. The number of   is greater than   The number
   degrees be-   is the same as   of degrees
   tween the fixed   is less than   between the
   points of Fahr-   fixed points on
   enheit's scale   Celsius' scale

c. The amount of   is greater than   The amount of
   heat we get   is the same as   heat we get
   from the sun   is less than   from the sun
   by convection   by radiation

d. The length of   is greater than   The length
   time the candle   is the same as   of time the
   burns in the   is less than   candle burns
   pint jar   in the quart jar

unit four
The Changing Earth

Men have not always been able to explain many of the natural events that take place on the earth. The word volcano comes from the name of the Roman god of fire Vulcan. Primitive people living on Pacific islands where volcanoes erupted thought that one of their gods was angry when a volcano began to erupt. The Pacific islanders had strange ceremonies in which they thought they would calm the angry god by sacrificing a beautiful young person to the volcano. The fact that the eruption sometimes did stop was only accidental. We know today that there is nothing we can do to stop an erupting volcano. The best we can do is observe carefully the various instruments that may signal a possible eruption and let people know so that they can prevent great loss of life and property. Today we know that volcanoes are caused by the release of molten materials from beneath the surface of the earth's crust. We do not have to rely on the explanation that a god is angry to explain this spectacular natural event.

On your way to school you may have passed streets and sidewalks, trees and lawns. Do you think any of these things have changed? Will they?

You might see that dirt has been blown into the street or that soil from a lawn has washed across a driveway. You may find places where the sidewalk is cracked. What could have caused it to crack?

Is the surface of the earth today exactly the same as it was yesterday? We have many reasons for believing that the earth was much different thousands of years ago. Scientists who study the uncovered remains of ancient cities are called archaeologists (ahr-kee-ahl-uh-jihsts). These cities have been buried for thousands of years by layers of soil. Such places give us a record not only of what these cities were like, but also what the surface of the earth was like.

WHAT CHANGES CAN WE SEE
ON THE EARTH?

The photograph shows many different features of our earth's surface. Some of these are ones you notice everyday. Hills, for example, are parts of the earth's surface you might often see. Rivers and mountains are familiar features. What other features can you name in the photograph? Have you seen some of them close to your home or during a vacation?

You may have noticed changes in lawns, streets or sidewalks. Other changes cannot be noticed from day to day, because they happen so slowly. A small hill may have once been a mountain. A stream could have been a great river. While some valleys are being filled by lakes, some flat lands may be carved into valleys. Such changes would take thousands, even millions, of years. Many features of the earth's surface change, but they do so ever so slowly.

1/Infer

Here is one change you can see in a short time. After boiling a small piece of marble rock in vinegar for about 10-15 minutes, remove the marble from the vinegar with a long-handled wooden spoon. Cool the piece of marble rock on a strip of paper towel. Examine it carefully after it has cooled. **How was** the marble changed? Was something new formed? What do you think caused the change? Remember you used an indicator called litmus paper to test liquids last year.

221

Vinegar is an acid and it reacts with marble. There are acids formed in the earth's surface. What might they do to pieces of rock? ■

The next activity will help you observe the effect of cold temperature on water.

2/Compare

Fill a small jar to the top with cold water. Put the cap on tightly and wrap the jar in a plastic bag. Close the end of the bag with rubber bands. Put the jar in a freezer. Let it stand overnight.

The next day remove the jar from the freezer and unwrap it carefully. If you do not have a plastic bag for this activity, put the jar in a large can without a lid. How has the jar of water changed? What do you think caused the change? Think of ways that cold causes other substances to change. ■

3/Compare

Cut a V-shaped notch in one end of an aluminum foil pan. Fill the pan with moistened soil. Place it in another larger pan; then raise the uncut end by resting it on a wooden block. Take a popsicle stick and starting at one end, rule lines 1/2″ apart on the stick. Color the spaces in this order: red, orange, yellow, green, blue and purple. Fasten the stick next to the V-shaped notch, with the red portion at the top as shown in the drawing. Each day for one week, pour one-half cup of water on the soil from the raised end.

What have you found out after observing your results for one week? Weigh any soil that has been washed into the larger pan. How many cups of water did you use? If more water was used, would your results have changed? Try tilting the pan more and continuing the activity for a longer time. Compare your results with the first ones. ▪

The kinds of changes you see correspond to bigger changes on the earth's surface. Few big changes on the surface of the earth take place rapidly. Most of them are the result of small ones taking place daily.

4/Observe

Heat a small piece of some rock, such as sandstone, limestone, or sidewalk cement, on a hot plate for about five minutes. Drop the heated rock into a metal can of cold water. How did the rock change? What might have caused any change? Can you now suggest one reason why a crack may appear in the sidewalk? ■

The next two activities will help you observe another way that the surface of the earth may be changed in appearance.

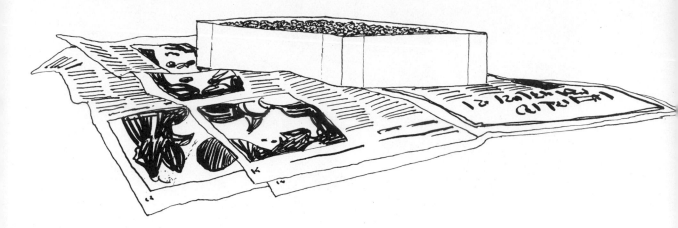

5/Observe

After filling a shallow box with loose, dry soil, place it on a sheet of newspaper. Use a ruler to smooth the surface of the soil. Blow across the surface. How has the surface of the soil changed? ■

6/Compare

Now place the box on another sheet of paper. Sprinkle part of the soil with water. Again blow across the surface of the soil. What do you observe? How do people in various areas prevent the wind from doing too much damage?

How much soil is there on the first newspaper? Is there any on the second newspaper? How much? Compare the movement of wet soil and dry soil. Explain the reason for any difference between them. What might happen to dry soil in a windstorm? ■

The earth can be changed by water, wind, acid, and temperature. Which of the statements listed below best illustrates one of these ways:

changed by water   *changed by temperature*
changed by wind   *changed by acid*

At the bottom of the Grand Canyon is the Colorado River.

Sometimes during a period of frost, freezing water may push against the underside of tar roads to make bumps.

Sand dunes change shape.

Sometimes the earth is eaten away to make caverns.

226

HOW DOES WIND CAUSE CHANGES
ON THE EARTH?

Have you ever seen a man walking on a windy day? A man's hat can suddenly blow off on a windy day. He may have to run down the street to catch it.

Watch the flag on your school building on a windy day. Is it blowing out straight from the flagpole? On a windy day, leaves may suddenly swirl up into the air. Dust will fly about. Did you really see what knocked the man's hat off or what made the flag move or the leaves swirl?

By observing carefully, you can see objects that are moved or changed by wind. Everyone has heard the wind, but who has really seen it? Clothes flapping on a clothesline can show the presence of wind. You can see the effects of wind, but you cannot see the wind itself.

Wind is powerful. It can push over trees or a sailboat on a stormy ocean. It can be gentle and blow softly. Wind can move fast during a storm or slowly in a breeze. The next activity shows you the effects of air in motion.

7/Observe

Mark a square piece of paper as shown. Fold up on the solid lines and down on the dotted ones. Now attach a thread to the center of the paper. Hold the paper by the thread over a light bulb. What happens? Do you know the reason for it? ■

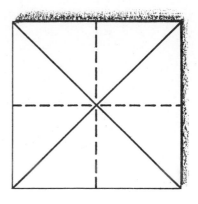

Air has weight. It can push. Air moves. Air moving over the surface of the earth is called wind. Do you think that the heat from the sun can change the movement of air?

Wind is always blowing somewhere on the surface of the earth. It can be a wild hurricane blowing more than 120 miles an hour or a mild breeze that just blows leaves across a lawn. Wind speeds can reach over 200 miles an hour. Most of the time wind is moving less than 15 miles per hour.

The force of wind causes changes in the surface of the earth. Some of them can be seen each day. Other changes take longer. A pile of dry leaves can be blown away in a few minutes. Wind blowing sand against a rock can take years to change the shape of that rock.

8/Measure

Use paper that is at least 20 inches by 30 inches. Mark off the paper into one-inch squares. Now tape the paper on a table in front of a fan. Put a table-spoonful of rice on the edge of the paper, just in front of the fan. Turn on the fan and when it reaches a steady speed, count to 15. Turn off the fan. Measure how far the rice moved across the paper. Record the

greatest distance the rice moved. Did all grains of rice move the same distance?

Now using a tablespoonful of puffed rice, repeat the activity. Record your observations. Next, you might use a larger fan. Is there any difference when the larger fan is used? Observe what happens and record your results. ■

9/Compare

Use a mixture of puffed rice and plain rice. Repeat the activity. Compare the distances the two kinds of rice moved.

Record your results when testing a tablespoonful of each of the following materials in the same way: dry soil, sand, salt, sugar, talcum powder. ■

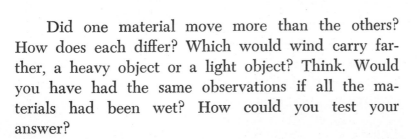

Did one material move more than the others? How does each differ? Which would wind carry farther, a heavy object or a light object? Think. Would you have had the same observations if all the materials had been wet? How could you test your answer?

In the 1930's the middle western United States had several years of very dry weather called a drought (DROWT). The drought destroyed farm crops. The soil dried out. Strong, dry winds blew the soil great distances. In 1934 a single windstorm blew an estimated 300 million tons of soil eastward to the Atlantic Ocean. Thousands of farms were ruined because their topsoil was carried away by the wind.

Suppose grass and other plants had been growing in the soil. Would less soil have been lost if there had been more rain? Think of some activities you could do to find out.

232

Wearing away of the earth by wind may cause the level of the land to become lower. During a long time period, the land level in southern Wyoming has dropped 150 feet. Wind carried dust and loose soil away. Compare your height with 150 feet. Measure 150 feet in the hall outside your classroom. Do you think that a lot of soil was moved in the 150 foot drop?

10/Measure

Measure changes in the depth of the sand if you live near a sandlot or beach. Mark one-inch lines on a strip of wood to use as a yardstick or use a ready-made one. Push one end of your measuring stick firmly into the sand. Record the reading.

Observe the level of the sand each day for three weeks or longer. Record your observations. ■

11/Compare

Compare the results you get after one week with those after three weeks. Suppose the record was kept for one year. What changes might you discover? Think of some of the causes for such changes. Why will the place where the stick is pushed into the sand make any difference in your findings? Predict if the sand level will be raised or lowered. ■

The wearing away of land by wind is called erosion (e-ROE-shun). Many deserts have been formed mostly by wind erosion. The first step in desert formation is the loss of grass and other plant life. When the topsoil dries up and its particles separate, the wind can carry it away. Once topsoil is gone, the wind continues to carry away the remaining dust, sand, and soil until sometimes only bare rock remains. This kind of change may take place in a few years.

Topsoil contains all the nutrients which the plant must obtain in order to grow. Topsoil is very important to the farmer. Without it he cannot grow food crops.

12/Compare

Repeat the activity with the V-shaped notch pan. This time use soil which has grass growing in it. How do your results compare? Can grass slow the erosion of soil by wind as well as water? ■

Sand or soil carried away by wind is deposited as the wind loses speed. The topsoil that wind picks up in one place may be deposited in another, thousands of miles away. Check the records you kept doing the activity with the two electric fans. Was there a difference in how far materials were moved with each fan?

Windblown topsoils often form rich farmlands, such as those in the Mississippi Valley. What else can cause the wind to deposit soil and other material that it carries?

13/Investigate

Set up the electric fan, the marked paper, and the grains of rice again. Place a chalkboard eraser at half the greatest distance the rice moved. Turn on the fan and count to 15. Turn off the fan. What did you observe? ■

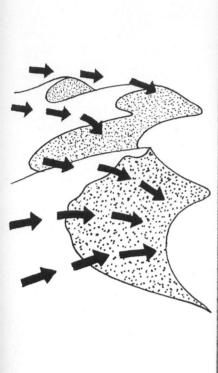

An object in the path of the wind will lessen its speed. This is the way huge piles of sand, called dunes, are formed. Sand grass can be used to keep the sand from blowing near the seacoast. Rocks and wooden slat fences lessen the speed of the wind. Such objects make the wind deposit some of the sand it may be carrying. A large dune builds up with a gentle slope on the side toward the wind. Examine a sand dune if possible. Figure out which side was toward the wind. Looking at the picture, decide the direction the wind was blowing when the dunes were formed. What happens to the shape of the sand dunes if the wind direction changes?

236

Wind-blown sand travels close to the earth. A rock is worn away as the sand blows against it. The wearing away of rocks and soil by wind and water is called weathering. The rocks in the photograph were changed in shape by the sand blown against them. Estimate how long it might have taken to shape these rocks. Could you predict what factors would determine how long the wearing away of the rock surface would take?

14/Compare

Take a piece of hard wood and rub it with rough sandpaper for one minute. Do this over a sheet of paper. Now use a piece of soft wood. Compare the amount of sawdust from each.

Use medium-weight sandpaper to rub a small piece of marble rock. Rub it 100 times and note your results. Use another piece of the same grade of sandpaper to rub a chunk of sandstone 100 times. Compare the two results. Explain the difference between the two kinds of rock. Repeat using 500 strokes. Compare the results. Suppose you had sanded each rock 1000 times. Predict how long it would take to wear away the rocks to dust. ■

When stone buildings become dark and dirty-looking, they are cleaned with air-blown sand. A high-speed stream of air and sand is blown at the surface of the building from a spray gun. This sandblasting quickly wears away the outer dirty layer of stone. The clean stone underneath is exposed.

Men who operate sand-blasting machinery must wear heavy protective clothing. Why is this safety measure necessary? Commercial sandblasting is a very rapid process. Compare it to sandblasting in nature. Are all rocks the same hardness? Which factors will determine how quickly the rocks are worn away?

239

With which of the following statements do you agree?

Wind changes the earth, but only by wearing it away.

Nothing can be done to stop or to slow the wearing away of the earth by wind.

Wind can be helpful as well as harmful.

Some of the earth's surfaces are more quickly worn away than others.

HOW DOES WATER CHANGE THE SURFACE OF THE EARTH?

Many changes in the earth's surface are caused by wind. But wind alone does not cause all change. About three-fourths of our earth is covered by water. Look around you. In what ways do you think water could change the surface of the earth?

The oceans of the world contain most of the earth's water. Water flows on and below the earth's surface to form springs, lakes, ponds, rivers and streams.

The heat of the sun evaporates water into the air surrounding the earth. Clouds form. Water returns to the surface of the earth as snow, rain, sleet, or hail.

Water leaving the surface of the earth and then returning to it is called the water cycle. All the earth's water is part of a water cycle.

When was the last rainy day? How long did it continue to rain? Is any of that rainwater still around? Watch the rain falling on the ground the next time it rains. Observe where it goes. Can you follow the water cycle?

15/Compare

First weigh an empty glass. Weigh it again after filling it with water. Explain the difference. ■

Gravity pulls water down as it does on all materials on the surface of the earth. Therefore, water has weight. Rain is pulled down to the earth by gravity. Some rain soaks into the earth. What happens to the rest of the rainwater? What happens to the water that soaks into the earth?

Fill a shallow pan with soil. Keep sprinkling the dirt with water until it cannot absorb any more. Put the pan in a larger one and tilt it slightly. Continue sprinkling. Observe what happens when more water falls than the soil can absorb. How does gravity affect water on the surface? Punch a hole in the bottom of the pan. Watch the water leak out of the hole. ■

There is a difference between water which runs off the surface of the soil and water which runs through the soil. Which do you think is of benefit to the plants?

Water running off a field or hill makes changes in the earth's surface. Where there is plenty of rain it wears away mountains and washes out valleys. Water is the main carver of the earth. It ruins good fertile soil by dissolving minerals and washing them away. Running water in nature is always on the move, wearing down and carrying away the earth's surface.

Running water moving from place to place, carries soil, sand, and other materials along with it. The surfaces over which water flows are carved by sharp-edged particles of rock and soil.

17/Observe

Put two tablespoonsful of soil in a pint jar of water. Shake the jar. What did you notice? Can you explain what you saw? ■

Water running off a mountainside forms swiftly flowing streams. Rocks and pebbles, caught up by the moving water smash against the stream beds and cut them away.

18/Investigate

Break a soft red brick with a hammer. Put several sharp pieces of the brick into a plastic container. Fill the container about half full with water. Screw on the top and place the container in a plastic bag in case it should break.

Have 10 friends shake the container 100 times each. Examine the brick pieces. What do you observe? What is the color of the water? Why? ■

19/Compare

Repeat the activity. Shake the container 1000 times each day for one week. Examine the contents of the container. What happens to rocks as thcy are carried along by fast moving streams? What do these rocks do to the sides of the streams? ■

246

Have you ever seen a valley with a stream or a small river winding through it? Such a valley may once have been level land as high as the surrounding hills. Earth materials that once filled the valley may have been carried away by the water, during many thousands of years.

The Grand Canyon of the Colorado River is one of the most amazing examples of river erosion. For 30 million years or more, the river has been cutting its way through a great plain of rock. It has carved a tremendous canyon that is 6000 feet deep in some places.

Another spot where erosion is always taking place is Niagara Falls. The Niagara River flows over a cliff of hard limestone and soft shale. The rock is being worn away at the rate of five feet per year by the moving water. Which rock would wear away faster? The shape of the falls has changed greatly because of this constant erosion. If you were to compare the shape of the falls today with a photograph taken 20 years ago, the changes could be easily seen.

Running water carries soil, bits of rocks and earth materials with it. As the swift moving streams broaden out, they flow more slowly. The stream deposits some of the earth materials. These materials, called sediments, gradually build up the river bottom.

Two or more rivers may join to form a river system. The largest one in our country is the Mississippi River system. Picking up earth materials in some places and dropping them in others, the Mississippi flows for more than 2300 miles. When it finally reaches the quiet waters of the Gulf of Mexico, the Mississippi deposits the last of its earth materials, over a million tons a day.

Most of the Mississippi's sediment is carried farther by the Gulf waters, but much is deposited to form a low plain where the river meets the sea. A plain built up at the mouth of a stream or river is called a delta. Pushing its way farther out into the Gulf of Mexico, the Mississippi delta continues to grow every day.

Deltas are built up as running water carries soil, bits of rock, and other earth materials with it. These substances are deposited on the bottom where the river broadens out and slows down. See for yourself what happens when a narrow, swift-flowing stream broadens out and flows more slowly.

20/Compare

Take a cupful of soil containing bits of rock, sand, and pebbles. Put the soil into a quart jar. Fill the jar almost to the top with water. Cover the jar tightly; shake it hard. Set the jar down and watch carefully as the earth materials settle.

Identify the material that drops to the bottom first. Which substance remains suspended in the water longest? Compare the differences between the materials. When running water loses speed which of the materials will be dropped first? Predict which materials will be carried farthest by the running water. ■

Have you seen washouts, gullies, or other changes made by rushing water? Wherever the ocean meets the land there is constant change. Sometimes the change is great and sudden such as when a single storm washes away part of an island. Usually the change is only a few shells or small amounts of sand washed back into the ocean or thrown up on the beach.

21/Discover

Place three sugar cubes in a small jar. Put the lid on tightly and shake the jar for a few minutes. Open it and examine the sugar cubes. Look at the corners of the cubes. What do you find at the bottom of the jar? ■

22/Predict

If you used pieces of sandstone what do you think you would find at the bottom of the jar? Where does sand come from? Most of the stones you find on a beach are smooth and rounded. Compare their shapes with those found in a backyard area. How does the action of waves change the shape? ■

Rocks are tumbled against each other as waves wash up on the beach. Gradually, the rocks on beaches are broken down into sand. The change from rock to sand does not occur overnight. Many thousands of years are needed to change a rocky coastline to an area of soft, rolling sand dunes. Predict which would take longer to change, a coastline of soft rock or one of hard rock, such as that found along the Maine coast.

23/Compare

Take a few pebbles and break them up into some pieces by wrapping them in a plastic bag and hitting them with a hammer. Examine a piece with a magnifying glass. Examine some clean sand with a magnifying glass. How does it compare to the rock pieces? ■

Rain falls on mountainsides, and runs off as a swift-moving stream. Streams join and form broad rivers that flow across plains and broad valleys to the ocean. All the way from falling rain to the sea, water is changing the earth's surface. How would a hard rain affect the soil by just striking it repeatedly?

Does all rain run off the land it falls upon? Plants would not be able to stay alive if this were so. Think what happens to water when someone waters a plant. Why do you often have to hill the earth around a plant? Where does the water go when a lawn or garden is watered?

24/Observe

Dip the end of a piece of paper towel into colored water. Note what happens. How far does the paper towel soak up the colored water? ■

254

Fill a sprinkling bottle with water. Now put a sponge on a sheet of wax paper and sprinkle it with water. Don't let any water run down the sides of the sponge. Continue sprinkling the sponge as long as water will disappear into it. Look at the sponge. Where does the water go? ■

The materials used in the activities retained water. Were all of them the same? Were they alike in any way?

Each of the materials used contained many empty spaces. Such materials are said to be porous (PAWR-us). Porous materials can soak up water and other liquids.

Is soil porous? Does it absorb water? Is more water absorbed by some soils than others? Name some other materials of the earth that soak up water.

26/Compare

Weigh pieces of a very hard rock, like marble or granite, and a very soft one like sandstone. Place both rocks in a jar of water. After soaking them overnight, wipe them dry. Weigh the pieces of rock again. Compare the differences between the dry rocks and the rocks which soaked overnight. What did you find out? Do all rocks soak up the same amount of water? ■

Layers of soil differ in the way they are able to hold water. The next activity will help you to see how water travels through different underground areas.

27/Describe

Fill a jar with layers of dry soil, small pebbles or rock chips, sand, coarse clay soil, and fine topsoil. Begin with the dry soil, as the picture shows, then build your layers to within two inches of the top of the jar. These layers are similar to the ones making up the crust of the earth. Now pour enough water onto the top layer to cover it well. Examine the jar after a few hours.

Explain what has happened to the water. Add more water, but be careful not to let any water stay above the top layer of soil. What happens now? What happens to rainwater when it falls on the earth's surface? ■

Water from the surface of the earth slowly collects underground. Do the next activity to observe the action of underground water.

28/Observe

Put a smooth round jar in the center of a deep pan. Fill the pan with sand. Pack down the sand and smooth out the surface. Pour water slowly on the sand until all of it is wet.

Wait a few minutes, then lift the jar carefully with a slow twisting motion. Watch the hole formed by the jar. Note what happens after a short time. Where does the water come from? Explain how it moves through the sand. How does this underground water fill wells? Explain why wells often go dry when there is no rain for a very long time. ■

The continual action of water on the earth's surface causes it to change. Do the next activity to help you understand how this occurs.

29/Explain

Fill a glass baking dish half-way with soil. Scoop some of it out of the center. Pack this soil against the sides to form a "valley" and two "hills". Now pour water gently on the soil. Keep packing the soil so it doesn't slide into the valley. Look through the sides of the dish and watch the water rise in the soil. Note what happens in the valley. This can help you explain how underground water helps to form streams and rivers. What happens to rivers and streams during a long dry period? ■

Some of the minerals in rocks are dissolved by underground water. Gases as well as these dissolved minerals slowly wear away the underground rocks. Underground water often hollows out large caves in the earth. If you have ever visited a cave, describe it for the class.

30/Observe

Put a tablespoonful of salt into a glass of warm water. Stir the water until all the salt is gone. Now the salt has been dissolved by the water. ■

A material able to dissolve others is called a solvent. Water is a solvent for many materials. Name others beside salt that dissolve in it.

31/Describe

Fill a glass with water. Let it stand for 30 minutes. Describe what you see on the insides of the glass. Where does this come from? Do you think air dissolves in water? ■

The next activity will help you to see another way that water causes rocks to change. Such changes take place over a long period of time.

32/Observe

Some rocks contain iron. Do water and oxygen from the air affect iron? Place an iron nail or tack on a wet sponge. Leave it there for one week. Add water to the sponge when it dries out. Observe what happens to the nail or tack. Try scraping its surface. ■

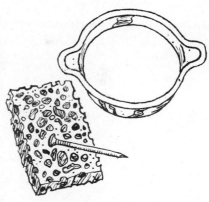

Rocks that contain iron will rust. Rust weakens the rock. The carbon dioxide in the air also dissolves in water. It forms an acid that dissolves certain rocks in the earth. The marble rocks that you boiled in vinegar were changed by an acid. Could such acids also change rocks in nature?

Below are two columns. The first lists activities like the ones given to you to do. The second lists what water can do to the earth. Which of the statements of Column A is the best example of the statements in Column B?

A

Tilt a pan of loose soil five inches. Pour water down the soil. What happens?

Fill a jar halfway with soil, and fill the remainder with water. Shake for thirty seconds. What happens to the soil when it stops moving?

Using a hand lens, compare pieces of broken pebbles with some rock.

Weigh a hard rock and a soft one. Soak both in water overnight, and compare their weights.

B

Land is built up at the mouth of a river.

When water runs off a hill, the earth's surface can be eroded.

Different kinds of rock and soil can hold different amounts of water.

Waves which crash rocks into other rocks can eventually make sand of them.

HOW DOES TEMPERATURE
CAUSE CHANGE?

The temperature differences over the earth's surface cause noticeable changes. After a long, cold winter you can see some of these changes. Try to remember some you may have seen and think of what might have caused them to occur.

33/Explain

Fill two half-pint cartons with water. Measure them to be sure they are the same size. Put one of the cartons in the freezer, until the water is frozen solid. Take the carton of ice from the freezer and compare it with the carton of water. Are the two cartons still the same size? ■

Most materials contract as they cool. Water is an exception to this rule. As water cools, it first contracts. Then, as it nears the freezing point, it expands. This expansion is so great that the ice takes up about 1/9th more space than the water did. If you want to test this you can place some water in a glass, mark the height, and then put it in the freezer at home. See if the ice, when it is formed, is higher than the mark you made on the glass.

Rocks with spaces in them can take in water. In cold weather, the water freezes and expands, causing the rocks to break and crumble into smaller pieces. Gradually, the rocks are broken down into soil for plants.

34/Compare

Take several pieces of porous sandstone. Soak them in a jar of water overnight. Place the stones in a plastic bag in the freezer of your refrigerator the next day. Examine the bag of stones one day later. How has the sandstone changed? ■

The upper slopes of most high mountain ranges, such as the Rocky Mountains, the Sierra Nevadas, and the Alaska Range, are white with snow all year. Snow sometimes lies hundreds of feet deep in protected hollows on these mountains. The top surface of the snow is soft, but toward the bottom it is packed to icy hardness by the weight of the snow above. These masses of snow are called snow fields.

If the snow doesn't melt in summer, the snow fields grow larger each winter. The snow-and-ice mass will begin to move downhill when its weight becomes great enough. A glacier (GLAY-sher) has started.

Glaciers, which carve the earth's surface, are slow-moving rivers of ice. Just how the glaciers move is not fully understood. Gravity helps the glaciers move downhill. But how do these solid, icy masses manage to turn corners and even to creep uphill at times? Again, we don't have the answer to this question.

266

35/Think

Take a tray of ice cubes, two square pieces of cardboard, and a brick. Place two groups of four ice cubes each on a table top. Put a cardboard square on top of each group of ice cubes. Now place the brick on top of one group of ice cubes. Time which ice cubes melt faster. Do you think pressure has anything to do with melting? ■

36/Compare

Take four ice cubes and place them in pairs, so that a book can be balanced on top. Let the book stay for a few minutes. Examine the ice cubes. What has happened? Compare this time with the brick. ■

Ice at the bottom of a glacier will melt because of the weight of the upper layers. According to one theory, the continuous process of melting, refreezing, and melting again somehow helps glaciers in their movements. However, this process appears to be more complicated than just melting and refreezing.

Glacial movement, though not completely understood, can be measured. Some glaciers move a few inches a year, others almost 100 feet each day. Most glacial movement is very slow, but glaciers are still very powerful in shaping the surface of the earth.

As the bottom and sides of a glacier melt and refreeze, the glacier picks up soil, sand, small rocks, and even huge boulders. Such earth materials become frozen in the edges of the moving glacier. When rock rubs against rock and soil, surfaces wear down.

268

Press an ice cube into a dish of sand. When it starts to melt, put the dish and the ice cube into the freezer for one hour. Take the ice cube out and see if it has picked up some of the sand. (If not, let the ice cube melt and refreeze it.) Now rub the sandy ice cube on a painted board. Note any change. ■

Glaciers, carrying earth materials, grind away at rocks and soil under them and along their sides. River valleys through which they travel are deepened and widened. Rock on mountainsides is scoured and scratched. Land once covered by a glacier would show the marks of this rubbing. What could you find in a stream flowing from a melting glacier?

While glaciers are always growing from their sources in the snow fields, they are always melting at their lower ends. A glacier will melt away entirely, if it melts faster than it can grow. When glaciers melt, much of their earth materials are deposited.

A melting glacier may often leave a great pile of earth materials it has gathered at the foot of a valley. Such materials then act as a dam, keeping back the water from the melting glacier. A lake is formed as water fills the valley.

Streams flowing from melting glaciers also deposit earth materials. Ice can carry heavy materials such as boulders, but its melting water carries only the finer, lighter earth materials such as sand and soil. In areas where these finer materials are deposited, large hills are formed.

Several times during the past million years North America and Europe were covered with huge sheets of ice, more than a mile thick. Many glaciers on the earth today are the remains of those great ice sheets.

Great ice sheets still bury the land masses of Greenland and Antarctica. Such glaciers are so large that if they were to melt, the sea level would rise more than 200 feet. Many of our cities would be flooded.

38/Think

Could you say that we are still in the Ice Age or that it passed thousands of years ago? Might we be at the beginning of a new Ice Age? Think what changes a new Ice Age might make in the earth's surface. ■

TESTING YOUR IDEAS

Do you agree with the following statements?

Glaciers grind away at mountains and carry boulders and soil.

Glaciers make streams, lakes, and hills.

It is mostly the temperature at which water freezes and melts which causes glacial changes.

HOW COULD MOUNTAINS BE MADE?

We know that water, wind, and glaciers can wear away mountains. We also know that this erosion has been taking place for a very long time. Why shouldn't the earth be a flat plain? How is it possible that there are mountains? Must we not say that the surface of the earth is rising as well as being worn away? Can we show that the surface of the earth in fact has been pushed up? The following activity will begin to help you answer these questions.

39/Observe

Fill a large pan half full of plaster of paris. Fill the remainder of the pan with water and stir carefully until it is as smooth as cake batter. Drop in shells, fish bones, crab claws, and bits of coral. Put the pan aside until the plaster dries. When it is completely dry, break it apart and observe the "fossils." ■

Fossils of ancient sea animals have been found in rocks of very high mountains. Therefore, does not this fact tell us that land once under the sea might have been pushed up in some way to make mountains? What might be one kind of push needed to make mountains?

40/Compare

Lay several pieces of brightly-colored blotting paper in a pile. These layers will represent rock layers. Placing your hands firmly on the ends of the pile, slowly bring your hands together. Watch carefully as you push. What happens? Does the blotting paper begin to bulge or rise? Compare the blotting paper with the layers in the photograph. Do you think that mountains are uplifted quickly or slowly? ■

Geologists (jee-AHL-uh-jishts) are scientists who study the changing earth. They believe that the land at the base of some mountains was once further apart.

Some points of land once 81 miles apart in the Appalachian mountains in Pennsylvania are now only 66 miles apart. What happened to the distance between your hands as you pushed the ends of the blotting paper together? Did the distance "shrink"? Do you think a shrinking earth can make mountains? Some geologists think it may be so.

The kind of mountain suggested by your activity is called a folded mountain. It is a bend in the earth's crust. Some rocks may bend. But can you imagine that some rocks may break to form mountains? Do the following activity to find out how this might happen.

41/Compare

Get some modeling clay which will dry out. Mold the clay into a piece one-half inch thick, six inches long, four inches wide. With your teacher's help, cut the clay along its width into two equal pieces. Make sure the cut is on a slant and does not go through the clay entirely. Turn the clay over to hide the cut and let the clay dry for an hour. Then, press down with one hand

along the cut and push the other half of the clay towards the cut. What does the cut represent? Does the clay begin to crack at the cut? After you have pushed, is one side of the clay higher? ■

Pressures can push up large volumes of rock as blocks along weaknesses or cracks in the earth's crust. These cracks, called faults, go deep in the earth's crust. Mountains pushed up along a fault are called block mountains. A sidewalk broken by tree roots growing underneath it is a tiny example of the way block mountains may have formed. But once the mountain is raised above the earth's surface, what do you think begins to happen? Might weather begin to erode the mountain and change its appearance after many years? The Sierra Nevada mountains shown in the picture are block mountains. Do you think they have been worn away by water, wind, and ice?

276

While the earth's surface may fold or fault, is it possible that it can also be pushed up from underneath the crust? As you will see in the next lesson, a part of the inside of the earth is magma, a thick, "syrup-like" rock that has melted. Find out if a fluid can push up a mountain by doing the next activity.

42/Compare

Place several layers of modeling clay softened with warm water over a balloon. Blow into the balloon. While air is not liquid like melted rock, it is still a fluid and can cause a push. What happens to the layers of soft clay as you blow the balloon up? ■

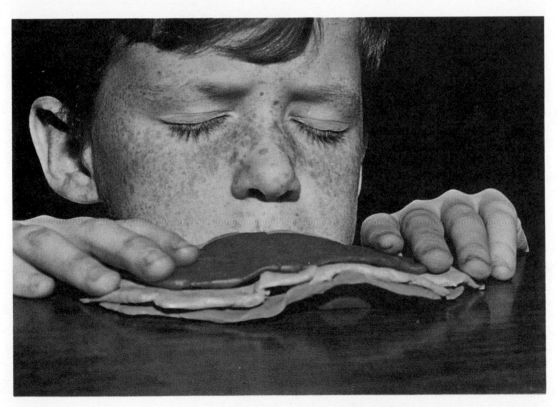

Liquid rock seeping between rock layers in the earth may raise the layers up. Mountains formed when liquid rock causes a lifting push are dome mountains. When the melted rock cools slowly under the earth's surface, the rock formed is very hard and durable. When weather wears away the surface layers of rock, the hard and durable rock is exposed.

You know that the earth's crust must be pushed in some way to form a mountain. But what causes the push? Is the earth shrinking? Or is the rock beneath the crust moving in some way to cause the crust to fold, fault, or rise? The questions suggest possible explanations, but geologists are not yet sure.

Which of the following kinds of mountains may have been produced by the causes found below?

block mountain
fold mountain
dome mountain

Large volumes of rock separated by faults may be pushed up by pressures in the earth's crust.

The pressure of magma under the crust may push up large areas of earth.

A mountain may rise because the earth's crust bends.

HOW DOES THE EARTH CHANGE SUDDENLY?

Most changes in the earth's surface come about slowly. There are other changes that can take place suddenly and violently. Late one Friday afternoon in 1964, the people of Alaska were going about their normal activities. Some were shopping, some were still at work, and others were getting ready for dinner.

Suddenly the earth began to shake. The ground cracked, and sections of it dropped several feet. Buildings crumbled and fell. Cars bounced around like rubber balls. The disturbance caused great waves in the Pacific Ocean that smashed shoreline cities along the Alaskan coast. Some effects from these waves were felt even in California, 2000 miles away.

These were not the kinds of changes usually made by water, wind, or ice. What caused this great change in the surface of the earth?

43/Observe

Hold a stick by the ends. Bend it until it breaks. What must you do if it doesn't break immediately? The stick can withstand a certain amount of force. It breaks when you exert more force than the stick can withstand. ■

The earth's rocks are subject to many forces. They break and shift when these forces become more than they can withstand. When rocks break and shift, this movement causes vibrations. These vibrations of the earth are called an earthquake.

Earthquakes most often occur along faults in the earth's crust. Rocks, deep in the crust, on either side of the fault, are being pushed in opposite directions. They begin to slide sideways against each other.

One great fault in the earth's crust located in North America is along the Alaskan coast. Another is in California. Probably the most serious earthquakes in our country would always be along these fault lines. Do other countries have these also?

Large landslides and volcanoes can also cause earthquakes. These disturbances are generally not as strong as those caused by the breaking and shifting of rocks. Even so, volcanoes and landslides can cause much damage.

44/Discover

Wrap a large rock in a cloth. Take it outside and break it with a hammer. Take two pieces of the rock that fit together and rub their edges together. Describe what you feel. ■

Vibration waves travel out in all directions from the place where an earthquake occurs. These waves can be recorded on a sensitive instrument called a seismograph (SYZ-ma-graf). Scientists can learn where the

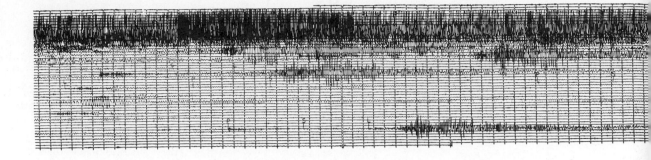

earthquake is taking place and how serious it is by studying seismograph recordings.

45/Observe

Put a dish or cup of water in the middle of a table. Fasten a flashlight to a support to hold it steady and aim it so that the light shines down at an angle on the water, as shown in the picture. Darken the room so that the light reflected from the water forms a spot on the wall. Now, rap the table gently and note the movement of the spot of light on the wall. Walk across

the floor near the table and note what happens. Jump up and down in the corner of the room away from the table. Describe what happens each time something moves in the room. Will your instrument pick up the vibrations of a truck going down the street? ■

Vibrations travel through the air, the floor, and the table every time something moves in the room. You might say that when you walk you are making a tiny earthquake. When these vibrations reach the water in the dish, they set up tiny waves on the water, and the reflected light begins to move. If the vibrations are weak the movement is small; if the vibrations are strong the movement is great. This is the way a real seismograph works, but, of course, it uses a recorder very much more complicated than a cup of water to detect the vibrations in the earth.

The numbers 1 to 12 are used to indicate the intensity of earthquakes. A reading between 8 and 9 on one such scale was made for the Alaskan earthquake of March, 1964. A reading of 1 would be a vibration almost unnoticed. Readings at the high end of the scale would be earthquakes causing great destruction and loss of life.

There are about 150,000 earthquakes a year. Most of them are so slight that we don't notice them. Earthquakes are happening all the time. They change the earth's surface in great and small ways.

In Hawaii, many people farm the fertile soil near the crater Kilauea (kee-low-AY-a). When the earth begins to tremble under their feet, the people know it may soon be time to move to another part of the island. Soon, hot lava may flow down the mountainside. It burns and buries everything in its path. The crater Kilauea is the mouth of the volcano.

Volcanoes are mountains formed by hot materials escaping from the earth's crust. Lava, steam, rocks, and hot gases may be thrown out by an erupting volcano. Kilauea has gently sloping sides since it gives off mostly liquid lava. Volcanoes giving off more solid material, such as ash and chunks of rock, have steeper sides.

Take a paper circle which measures 5 inches a-cross. Cut a slit from the edge of the circle to the center. Overlap the edges of the slit one inch to form a cone. Hold the overlapped edges in position with tape. Now put the cone upside down in the mouth of a jar. Use grass seed, sawdust, or wood shavings from a pencil sharpener to fill the cone. Lay a flat piece of cardboard over the cone's open end and tape the cone firmly to the cardboard. Make a hole in the cardboard, just big enough for a piece of rubber tubing. Pinch the tubing closed with a spring-type clothespin. Turn the cardboard over so the cone is on top and place it on two books, with space between them for the tubing, as shown in the drawing. Cut off the tip of the cone. Coat the outside of the cone with paper cement. Blow into the rubber tube until it is full of air. Remove the clothespin and keep blowing. This model is like a volcano that has already been formed and is erupting again. You can see how an eruption increases the size of a volcanic mountain. ■

It was February 20, 1943. A Mexican farmer heard a rumbling noise in the earth, and smoke began to rise out of the ground. He ran into the village to tell his neighbors. The birth of a volcano had begun. The next day his cornfield was gone. In its place stood a cone 100 feet high, pouring out clouds of smoke and ash. Small earthquakes shook the ground for weeks. Rocks and ash were blasted high into the air. The cone continued to grow. Lava poured out of cracks that appeared in the earth.

When the erupting stopped in 1952, the volcano was 1350 feet high. It was called Paricutín (pa-REE-koo-teen), after the nearby village that it buried. Today the volcano is quiet, but it may waken again.

Sometimes volcanoes destroy their cones instead of making them higher. Paricutín blasted away parts of its cone in some of its explosions.

Krakatoa (kra-ka-TOW-a) was an East Indian island that had begun as a volcano on the ocean floor. It grew slowly until its cone towered high above the sea. In 1883, it blasted itself to pieces in a series of eruptions. The crumbled remains of the island collapsed into a great hole in the ocean bottom. A small new cone is building now where Krakatoa once stood. Someday there may be a repeat performance.

47/Observe

Set up the cardboard and rubber tubing again. You won't need the paper cone this time. Pinch the

rubber tubing closed. Make a mound of seeds or shavings over the opening of the tube. Remove the clothespin. Note what happens as you blow through the tube. ■

Volcanic action is not always spectacular. Lava sometimes flows out onto the earth's surface from long cracks. Such lava flows more gently than lava that has had to force its way through a small opening.

Many of the earth's regions have been covered by lava flowing from long cracks. A hilly part of Iceland was changed to a high level mound by such a lava flow. The Columbia and Snake River Plateau in the western United States was formed by lava flows.

48/Describe

Fill a cake pan with runny mud. Cut a piece of heavy cardboard to fit the pan. Now make two slits in the cardboard, 6 inches long and 1/4 inch wide. Press the cardboard down into the loose mud. Describe what happens. ■

Volcanic action builds and destroys mountains. Undersea volcanoes build up volcanic islands and sometimes destroy them, as in the case of Krakatoa. Hilly regions can be changed to high, flat plateaus by flowing lava.

Magma and lava cool to form rocks. Such heat-formed rocks are called igneous (IG-nee-us). Granite and basalt are examples of igneous rocks. Volcanic ash hardens to form a rock called tuff. Soil that forms from tiny pieces of volcanic material is very fertile. It makes excellent farmland.

Volcanoes also give off water vapor and carbon dioxide. In the early days of the earth's formation water vapor given off by volcanoes condensed and helped to fill the oceans. Plants could not live without carbon dioxide in the atmosphere. So you see that although volcanoes can cause great destruction, they have helped make the earth suitable for living things.

TESTING YOUR IDEAS

Which of the statements given below are about earthquakes, volcanoes, and erosion? Which are only about earthquakes and volcanoes? Which are only about erosion?

The earth can change.
The earth can change slowly.
The earth can change quickly and with little warning.
Changes in the earth can sometimes be controlled.

HOW DOES MAN CHANGE THE EARTH'S SURFACE?

When the first colonist arrived in what is now called the United States, he found great forests extending from the Atlantic Ocean to the Mississippi River. Today, as we fly over this same land, we see large cities, many towns and villages and some forest land. Man, too, changes the surface of the earth and he has not always been careful in how he did it.

There was so much forest land that man was careless in how he cut down the trees and he did not plant new ones. Topsoil was washed away. It poured into the streams so that sewer systems overflowed and also poured into the streams. Great destruction to land, property, and life resulted.

Today man has learned to save the forests by more careful cutting of trees and replanting of forest land.

49/Observe

Find a place where new houses are being built. What changes in the earth's surface do you observe? Examine any water run-off from the land. What do you notice? ■

Farmlands and forest areas must be used carefully. Soil and forest conservation must be practiced not only to preserve the land from erosion, but also to preserve living places for animal life.

Man has changed the earth's surface by changing the surroundings of living things. He has learned to use many chemicals to keep plants from being destroyed by insects and disease. Do you remember what happened to the salt that was dropped into the glass of water? What do you think happens to many of the chemicals on the plants as the rain falls on the plants and washes the chemicals off?

Many of these chemicals, called insecticides, are poisonous to fish, birds, or animals that drink from the streams.

Sewage is allowed to drain off into lakes and seas. As our cities have grown, our streams have become dangerous to drink from and swim in, and they have changed in appearance.

50/Observe

If you live near a stream or lake, do you find evidence of man's use or abuse? ■

Where does the water supply come from? Find out how it is made safe for you to drink. If you have a swimming pool in a nearby public park, find out what is done to keep the water safe to use. ■

The age of the earth is figured in billions of years. The landscape you see today is only a moment in the long history of the changing earth.

The ocean waves may plunge massive cliffs into the sea overnight. A volcano may build up a high mountain in a week or month. But most changes in the earth's surface come about gradually, during hundreds of thousands or millions of years.

Ages from now, there may be high mountains where you see only hills today. The great mountain ranges of the earth today may have vanished ten million years from now. Over the ages of time, the surface of the earth is built up in some areas and worn down in others. Tell what you know about the changing surface of the earth that you can see about you.

TESTING YOUR IDEAS

Helen and Bud were discussing how man had changed the earth's surface. Helen said that the changes were all for the best. Bud disagreed. Helen said that man had built cities, towns, and villages. He had also turned forests and plains into useful farmland. In addition, man had built canals and waterways to make travel easier. Dams had been built to give man enough water.

Bud said that man had not learned to change the earth's surface usefully. He had spoiled rivers, streams, and lakes with sewage and dangerous chemicals. He had cut down entire forests without reseeding. As a result, the beauty of the land was spoiled. Rains also washed away the soil once held in place by roots. All of this damage disturbed and in many cases destroyed wildlife.

With which point of view, Helen's or Bud's, do you agree? Do you think that to combine their views in some way would be best?

Below are listed particular statements about the changing earth and general statements about it too. Which of the particular statements about the changing earth are contained in the general statements? A general statement may explain more than one particular statement.

Particular Statement

1. Ice can break up rocks.

2. Land once below the surface of the sea is now above it.

3. A large fault area in the United States lies on the coast of California.

4. Planting grass can prevent erosion.

5. A glacier sometimes makes at its foot a hill or lake.

General Statement

A. Wind can carry away dry topsoil and deposit it elsewhere.

B. Water can wear away land and deposit it elsewhere.

C. Freezing and melting water can erode rocks.

D. Glaciers cause the earth's surface to change.

E. Pressures in the earth can cause changes in the surface.

296

Particular Statement

6. In 1934, a single windstorm blew about 300 million tons of soil from the midwestern United States to the Atlantic Ocean.

7. In Alaska late one Friday afternoon in 1964, the ground cracked, and sections fell several feet.

8. The rock of Niagara Falls is being worn away five feet a year.

9. If trees are cut down and not replaced, harsh rains can wear away forest topsoil.

10. Land built up at the mouth of a river is called a delta.

General Statement

F. Sometimes a volcano or earthquake can change the earth's surface quickly.

G. Man can change the earth's surface.

John and Edward were talking about how the earth had changed. Both students agreed that the forces which were changing the earth today were the forces which changed it in the past. John, however, thought that the changes could not have been very great. After all, how could streams, winds, and glaciers wear down mountains? Edward said that in northern Wisconsin, Michigan, and Minnesota there were only the "roots" of what were once great mountains. Edward said that streams, winds, and glaciers had worn these mountains down. John laughed, "Impossible." "Streams and things are too weak. How could they cause great change?" "Simple," said Edward. "It's a one word answer—time!"

What do you think Edward meant by his answer?

Keep a scrapbook of all sorts of unusual occurrences such as earthquakes, volcanic eruptions, new volcanoes, tornadoes, hurricanes, and severe ice storms that you can find in the daily newspapers. Keep this for at least four months and possibly even one year.

Find an area near your home that shows erosion and try to discover how it occurred and what preventative measures could have been taken. Can you do anything about it now to stop the erosion?

Find out how seacoast areas prepare for the damage that wind and water do to these regions during the winter. Write to the Department of Interior, Washington, D.C. and see what information you can get about the prevention of erosion from our seacoast areas.

Make a collection of different types of rocks and soil and find about as much information about the rocks and soil as you can from various sourcebooks.

GLOSSARY

absorbed heat (ab-SORBD HEET)   heat that sinks into some surfaces

air sacs (AIR SACKS)   balloon-like sacs where oxygen and waste materials are exchanged

air tubes (AIR TUBZ)   branches of the windpipe that carry air to the air sacs

armadillo (AR-muh-DILL-oe)   small burrowing animal whose head and body have a hard bony covering

artery (ART-uh-ree)   a blood tube that carries blood away from the heart

balanced diet (BAL-unst DIE-uht)   a diet that gives the healthy amounts of each food group

beriberi (BER-ee-BER-ee)   a disease caused by a lack of vitamin B

block mountain (BLOK moun-tin)   a mountain formed by the uplifting of a large area of the earth's crust

body system (SIS-tem)   the parts of an organism that work together to carry on a life activity

bread group (BRED GROOHP)   an important food group that includes breads, cereals, and cakes and should be included in a daily diet

capillary (KAP-i-ler-ee)   a tiny blood tube that gives up digested food materials and oxygen to the cells and picks up waste materials from the cells

carbohydrates (cahr-bo-HIE-drayts)   food that contains sugar and starch and provides a good source of energy

cartilage (KAR-ti-lij)   a rubbery tissue that makes up most of an infant's skeleton

cells (SELLZ)   the smallest units of living matter that make up the body

Celsius scale (SELL-see-us SKALE)   a thermometer scale on which the freezing point of water is marked 0° and the boiling point of water is 100 °

chemical change (KEM-i-k'l CHANJE)   when a material is broken down and one or more new substances are formed

conduction (kun-DUCK-shun)   the way heat travels through solids

contract (kun-TRAKT)   to decrease in size

convection currents (Kun-VECK-shun KUR-entz) upward and downward movement of a fluid because of changes in heating.

crust (KRUST)   the earth's outer layer which is make up of soil, rocks, and minerals

delta (DELL-tuh)   a low plain at the mouth of a river or sea, built up by the settling out and accumulation of sediment

density (DEN-sa-tee)   the weight of a unit volume

desert (DEZ-ert)   a region with little rainfall and often very little life

diaphragm (DIE-uh-fram)   a large muscle directly under the ribs that controls breathing

diet (DIE-uht)   all the food that you eat every day

digestion (di-JES-chun)   process by which the body changes food into a form that can be used

dispersal (dis-PER-sal)   all the ways in which seeds are carried to different places

dome mountain (DOME MOUN-tin)   a mountain formed by upward pressures beneath a weak spot in the earth's crust

dormancy (DAWR-mun-see)   a period of seasonal inactivity in certain plants

drought (DROWT)   several years of very dry weather

dune (DOOHN)   a huge pile of sand formed by the wind

energy (EN-ur-jee)   the ability to do work

erosion (ee-ROE-zhun)   the wearing away of the earth's surface by water, wind, and ice

estivation (ess-tuh-VAY-shun)   a resting state that some animals go into during the summer

expand (eck-SPAND)   to increase in size

Fahrenheit (FAR-en-HITE)   a thermometer scale on which the freezing point of water is marked 32° and the boiling point of water is marked 212°

fats (FATS)   food found in butter, lard, egg yolks, and bacon and provides a good source of energy

fault (FAWLT)   a deep break in the earth's crust caused by stress and pressure

fluids (FLOO-idz)   a name for liquids and gases

folded mountain (FOLD-ed MOUN-tin)   a mountain formed by the uplifting and wrinkling of the earth's crust

food chain (FOOD CHANE)   food relationships between plants and animals

fossil (FOSS-ul)   remains of ancient animals found buried in rocks

gas (GASS)   a substance which has no definite shape or volume; it expands to fill its container

glacier (GLAY-shur)   large mass of ice formed from snow in high, old mountains

glands (GLANDZ) organs which produce special body substances such as digestive juices and saliva

gravity (GRAV-uh-tee) pull of the earth that draws all objects on or near the earth toward its center

grub (GRUB) fat, white worms which are a stage in the development of a beetle

habitat (HAB-i-tat) the place where a plant or animal usually lives

heart (HART) a powerful muscle that pumps blood to all parts of the body

heart valve (HART VALV) fold of tissue in the heart that keeps the blood flowing in one direction

hibernation (hy-ber-NAY-shun) a resting state that some animals go into during the winter shown by sleeping, lowered body temperature and sluggishness

igneous rock (IG-nee-us ROCK) rocks formed from the heat of a volcano

insulators (IN-suh-LATE'rz) materials that are poor conductors of heat

kelp (KELP) large brown sea plants frequently found in the Pacific Ocean

large intestine (in-TESS-tin) an organ of digestion where water is taken back into the blood and waste materials are passed out of the body

life zone (LIFE ZONE) area of plant and animal life. On a mountainside, changes appear as different coloring in plants, as you climb.

liquid (LI-quid) a substance that has a definite volume but no definite shape; it takes the shape of its container

304

litmus paper (LIT-muss PAY-pur)   a chemical indicator used to test for acids and bases.

liver (LIV-uhr)   an organ that produces bile which aids in the digestion of fats

magma (MAG-muh)   melted rock materials below the surface of the earth; may flow from volcano

meat group (MEET GROOHP)   an important food group that includes meat, fish, and poultry and should be included in your daily diet

migrate (MY-grayt)   the movement of animals in large numbers from one place to a distant place

milk group (MILK GROOHP)   an important food group that includes milk, butter, cheese, cream, and ice cream and should be included in your daily diet

milt (MILT)   whitish fluid released from a male fish which fertilizes the eggs of the female fish

minerals (MIN-ur-uhlz) a food substance that builds strong bones, hard teeth, and healthy blood

muscular system (MUS-kyoo-lur SIS-tem)   the muscles of the body that make the bones move

nervous system (NUR-vuhs SIS-tem)   the system that controls all of the body's activities

organism (OR-gan-izm)   any living thing whose parts act together as a unit

organs (OAR-gunz)   the different parts that make up the systems of organisms

pancreas (PAN-kree-uhs)   a large gland near the stomach which produces a digestive juice

physical change (FIZZ-i-k'l CHANJE)   when a material changes in appearance but remains the same material

plankton (PLANK-tun)   free-floating algae and microscopic animals found in water

plasma (PLAZ-muh)   the liquid part of the blood that carries digested food and waste materials

porous (PAWR-us)   materials that can soak up water and other liquids

protective coloration (pruh-TEK-tiv KUL-uh-ray-shun)   the blending of an animal with the color of its surroundings

proteins (PRO- teenz)   food that builds up and repairs body tissues

pulse (PULS)   the throb felt in a blood tube caused by the contraction of the heart muscle

radiation (RAY-dee-AY-shun)   when heat travels in all directions from a hot object

reflected heat (ree-FLECK-ted HEET)   heat that bounces off some substances

reflex action (REE-fleks ACK-shun)   an action that happens quickly and without our control

respiratory system (RES-puh-ruh-taw-ree SIS-tem)   the system which regulates the oxygen you breathe in and the other gases you breathe out.

sandstone (SAND-stone)   rock formed by particles that have been under great pressure.

scurvy (SKUR-vee)   disease caused by lack of Vitamin C

sediment (SED-uh-munt)   particles of rock and soil that settle to the bottom of a river

seismograph (SYZ-ma-graf)   a sensitive instrument that records the vibrations of an earthquake

skeletal system (SKEL-uh-t'l SIS-tem)   all the bones of an organism

small intestine (in-TESS-tin)   an organ of digestion where food is broken down and absorbed into the blood

spawning (SPAWN-ing)   the depositing of eggs by a female fish

stomach (STOM-uck)   an organ of digestion where food is mixed with digestive juices and begins to be broken down

terrarium (tuh-RAIR-ee-um)   a self-contained area for growing plants indoors and keeping small land animals.

thermometer (thur-MOM-eh-tur)   an instrument used to take temperature

timberline (TIM-bur-line)   a definite line on a mountain where the growth of trees stops

tissues (TISH-yooz)   the special material that makes up the organs of the body

topsoil (TOP-soyl)   a rich soil that contains all the nutrients which a plant needs in order to grow

vegetable group (VEJ-eh-tuh-bull GROOHP) an important food group that includes vegetables and fruit and should be included in your daily diet

vegetarian (veh-juh-TAIR-ee-unz)   animals that feed only on plants

vein (VAYN)   a blood tube that carries blood toward the heart

vitamins (VY-tuh-minz)   substances found in food that aid and regulate body activity and growth.

water cycle (WAH-tur SIE-kul)   movement of water from the earth's surface into the atmosphere and back again

water vapor (WAH-tur VAY-pur)   a gas formed when water is heated

weathering (WETH-ur-ing)   wearing away of rocks due to the action of wind and water over a long period of time

work (WURK)   movement of an object through a distance by force

INDEX

PHOTO CREDITS